A
Woman's
Secret *for*
Confident
Living

A Woman's Secret *for* Confident Living

KAROL LADD

HARVEST HOUSE PUBLISHERS

EUGENE, OREGON

Cover by Koechel Peterson & Associates, Inc., Minneapolis, Minnesota

Cover photo © Hemera / Thinkstock; back-cover author photo by Shooting Starr Photography, Cindi Starr, www.shootingstarrphotos.com

A WOMAN'S SECRET FOR CONFIDENT LIVING
Copyright © 2011 by Karol Ladd
Published by Harvest House Publishers
Eugene, Oregon 97402
www.harvesthousepublishers.com

Library of Congress Cataloging-in-Publication Data
Ladd, Karol.
A woman's secret for confident living / Karol Ladd.
   p. cm.
ISBN 978-0-7369-2965-3 (pbk.)
ISBN 978-0-7369-4217-1 (eBook)
   1. Christian women—Religious life—Textbooks. 2. Confidence—Religious aspects—Christianity—Textbooks. 3. Bible. N.T. Colossians—Textbooks. I. Title.
BV4527.L2535 2011
248.8'43—dc22
                                                                           2010051945

Printed in the United States of America
    11 12 13 14 15 16 17 18 19 / VP-SK / 10 9 8 7 6 5 4 3 2 1

*To every woman
who desires to experience
the joy of walking
in God-confidence
rather than self-confidence.*

A special thank-you to the tremendous Harvest House team, and to the numerous people who allowed me to share their stories in this book.

Contents

ℬold and Beautiful

*"May the God of hope fill you with all joy and peace
as you trust in him,
so that you may overflow with hope
by the power of the Holy Spirit."*

ROMANS 15:13

*"Choose to accept and become
the person God has made you to be."*

JOHN MASON

Confident? That's not exactly how I would have described myself for much of my life. No, words like *insecure* and *self-doubting* were much more accurate. For many years, even as a Christian, I battled self-defeating thoughts and guilt feelings in my mind. Perhaps you can relate to what I'm talking about in your own life. Most women struggle with some form of insecurity. Even women who appear confident on the outside often struggle internally with a lack of self-assurance. It's one thing to *look* confident; it's another to *be* confident. This book is all about discovering a rock-solid confidence in your heart and mind. The truths in this book have impacted my own life personally, and I believe they can make a powerful difference in your life as well.

At first glance it may seem like the focus of this book is on you, but it actually isn't completely about you. I know you would think a book about confident living would center on you and how you can become a more self-assured woman. And yes, as a result of reading this book I believe you will have a new inner confidence and a powerfully positive perspective on life, but I just don't want you to get the idea that this book is focused entirely on you. In all honesty, it is about God and the grace-filled love and purpose He has for your life. True and lasting confidence is found not in focusing on ourselves, but focusing on the One who created us and discovering our confidence in Him. He is the One who gives us the strength and power to walk boldly in this world.

The word *confidence* means to have a firm belief or trust. Its root word, *fidere,* means "faithful" or "faith" and is the same root you see in words like *fidelity* or *confidant.* To have confidence means you have faith or trust in someone or something. Now we can try to live our lives by placing our confidence in our appearance or a relationship, or in having the right job or enough money, or in being a good parent, but none of these can offer lasting security or inner strength. A *God-confidence* (faith in our Creator and Savior) is different. When we place our hope and security in Him, no one can take it away. It is a rock-solid confidence from the wellspring of our soul. How do we get to a place where we live with a God-confidence?

The apostle Paul said, "Let your roots grow down deep into Christ." He penned these words to the early believers living in Colossae (now in southwest Turkey) as he expressed the importance of knowing Christ and finding satisfaction and security in Him. The truth is, the entire book of Colossians can lead us to a greater understanding of who we are in Christ and how we can confidently interact with others. It is a unique book filled with wisdom and knowledge about our relationship with God. *A Woman's Secret for Confident Living* is a delightful and deliberate examination of the truths about God in Colossians, which can literally transform the way you see yourself and live your life.

Paul encouraged the Colossians to live boldly and confidently in Christ. He wanted them to know what they believed and then to live out those beliefs with a wholehearted passion. His desire was for them to experience a very real faith based on a relationship with Christ, not religion or rules. He hoped they would come to realize that all the treasures of wisdom and knowledge are found in Christ. These are my dreams and desires for you as well, as you read this book. Confidence begins in our thinking and what we believe, and it plays out through the way we live our life in relationship to others. Our confidence spreads its wings and soars when we realize that God has a purpose for our life, and as we use our gifts and talents for His glory.

What to Do with This Book

You can enjoy this book as you read it on your own, or you can work through it with a friend. You may want to gather several girlfriends together and use it for a group study. The first group book study I ever taught was in my own neighborhood, with women I hardly knew. I left flyers in mailboxes and hoped someone would show up. They did! We started our first neighborhood study with a handful of women from all different religious backgrounds and all different ages. The study offered a great way to meet my neighbors and to help women in their walk with Christ no matter where they were coming from. I encourage you to reach out to co-workers, neighbors, or acquaintances and invite them to read through this book with you. The title is inviting, and it offers a wonderful way to get to know each other and to search through spiritual truths together. You will discover that this study can be a real connector for you and your friends as you discuss the chapters together.

At the end of each chapter you will find a helpful section called "Confident Steps." It is a way for you to take what you have read and personalize it. It offers additional scripture to read if you want to dig deeper. In this section I have included a part called "Battle for the Truth," which offers a Confidence Builder and a Confidence Defeater (a false idea we tend to believe). It is important to recognize some of the lies that pop into our minds and wage war against our confidence, so I want to help you identify some of these thought patterns. You will also find a list of choices you can make as a result of the truth. Finally, the Confident Steps section ends with a deliberate plan, which is an action step to carry out what you have just learned in a practical sense.

I believe it is one thing to read a book, but another thing to personally apply it to our current circumstances. Confident Steps gives you the tools to help you make each chapter a little more real in your daily life.

Group study questions can be found at the back of the book. These are meant to help you stimulate meaningful discussions and to help build conversations about the scripture studied in each chapter. You can also use the coordinating six-session video series, which highlights the key points in the lesson. I think you may like the videos even if there are just a few of you as it will help you facilitate the study and hear additional information and stories. For me personally, the study of Colossians has not only deepened the foundation of my confidence in Christ, but it has also challenged me to build into the relationships in my life and to get rid of the negative thoughts and habits that plagued my thinking. I believe this study can have an equally powerful effect on your life, so let's begin the journey together and enjoy the blessings God has in store, one confident step at a time.

PART ONE

ransform Your Thinking

"I have chosen the way of truth;
I have set my heart on your laws.
I hold fast to your statutes, O Lord;
do not let me be put to shame.
I run in the path of your commands,
for you have set my heart free."

Psalm 119:30-32

"We know the truth, not only by the reason,
but also by the heart."

Pascal

$\mathcal{W}$here in the World Is Truth?

*"Do not conform any longer to the pattern of this world,
but be transformed by the renewing of your mind.
Then you will be able to test and approve what God's
will is—his good, pleasing and perfect will."*

ROMANS 12:2

*"What comes into our minds when we think about God
is the most important thing about us."*

A.W. TOZER

When our daughter told us she wanted to major in philosophy at college, I was a bit concerned. Philosophy? What does a person do in life with a philosophy degree? I pictured men with long hair and beards sitting around on stone benches discussing the meaning of life. Having never taken a philosophy class in all of my years of schooling, I wasn't quite sure what a degree in philosophy really looked like, so I went to the bookstore and picked up a few books on the topic. *Philosophy for Dummies* was actually my favorite—quite an insightful read and very helpful in my incredibly intellectual pursuit of understanding philosophy. Unfortunately, the books I read never did answer the question about what a person does in life with a philosophy degree, but at least I was able to carry on a slightly coherent conversation about the Socratic method with my daughter.

I do want you to know that our daughter's college experience had a positive outcome. During her years of study at Baylor University, she became increasingly sensitive toward the needs of the impoverished families in the city of Waco. More importantly, she recognized the common condition of the poverty of the soul (I think that's a philosophical term), and so she began to reach out and serve the children in her community through the connection of visual arts. She went on to start Waco Arts Initiative, an afterschool art program for the kids living in the government housing projects. There you have it—there's one perfectly wonderful thing you can do with a philosophy degree!

So what is the study of philosophy all about anyway? The term philosophy actually means the love of wisdom and knowledge. The Greek root word *philos* means loving and *sophos* means wise. In a broad sense, philosophy is an investigation into the principles and laws that regulate the universe. More specifically it refers to a system of belief or doctrine about truth, existence, natural laws, theology, and morality. Our personal philosophy colors the way we understand the world, how we think about ourselves and, most importantly, what we believe about God.

Thousands of years ago Socrates, Plato, and Aristotle made philosophical waves in their own community, and the ripple effects of their ideas are still felt today. Throughout the ages, philosophers concerned themselves with the existence of God and His influence on creation. In our postmodern culture it may seem like philosophy is distant and irrelevant, but the significance of knowing what we believe and why we believe it has never diminished. Our pursuit of wisdom and knowledge must be grounded in truth and not in the winds of current trends or popular ways of thinking. As we dive into Colossians, we find that the believers were battling the influence of popular philosophies of their day, and Paul was deeply concerned about their knowledge of the truth. He wanted them to know with certainty the truth about Christ. Paul wrote his letter to the Colossians in order to strengthen their understanding and philosophy of life based on Christ and the truth of God's Word. We too need to establish who we are and what we believe in order to develop a foundation for our confidence.

Colossal Confusion

Recently for my fiftieth birthday (and I can't believe I just told you my age) my husband, Curt, decided to take me on a celebration trip to Santa Fe, New Mexico. Have you ever been there? It is quite a cross section of people and beliefs. Although Christianity seems to have a strong presence, with several beautiful cathedrals in the square, New Age mysticism and Native American traditions also dominate the culture. The city is what I would call a bouillabaisse of philosophies and ideas. Now my friends always laugh at me when I use the word *bouillabaisse* because it's not a term people use every day. I perhaps overuse the word to describe anything filled with variety. Bouillabaisse is actually a French word that describes a stew or chowder made with several different kinds of fish. It's the perfect word to describe different concepts and ideas blended together in one place.

Interestingly, the city of Colossae back in Paul's day had some similarities to modern-day Santa Fe, as both cities seem to be Meccas of merging ideas. Oddly, both cities were known for their merging roads as well as their merging ideas. In its early years, Santa Fe served as a crossroads for two major trading thoroughfares: the Santa Fe trail, extending from Missouri to Santa Fe, and El Camino Real, which was a supply route from Mexico City. In a similar way, in the fifth century BC the city of Colossae was significantly situated at the junction of the main trade routes in Asia going east-west and north-south. By the time Paul came on the scene, the main roads had been rerouted to the nearby city of Laodicea, which led to the gradual decline of Colossae. The Colossians lost most of their commerce and industry, yet they still remained at the crossroads of philosophical ideas.

It's All About What You Believe

So what in the world does philosophy have to do with you and me and our lives today? It comes down to this—what we believe about

God affects how we function in this world. If we think of God as an angry and demanding dictator, then we function as fretful and hopeless slaves. If we see Him as a careless Creator who keeps His hands off what happens in our world, then we tend to see life as purposeless and haphazard, and ourselves as insignificant. Yet if we recognize God our Father as the High King of heaven and Creator of all, the One who cares about the details of our lives and sent His only Son to give His life on our behalf, then we value our lives as holy and dearly loved children. We also value the lives of other people as well.

If we want to live with confident hope, then we must be firmly established in our philosophy of God. We must know what we believe about Him. Typically, I'm not a big watcher of television reality shows, but one show recently caught my interest. The premise of the show is built around the CEO or president or head honcho of a major corporation working incognito in the lower ranks of their business. Picture this: the CEO of a national waste management company cleaning out porta-potties with the service guys, or a president of a popular hamburger chain flipping burgers at the restaurant. Usually the boss returns to the corporate offices with a great appreciation for what the workers do day in and day out, and they also begin to implement changes and improvements in the field.

My favorite part of the show is at the very end, when the field personnel are called into the corporate offices and are told the truth about the identity of their mysterious co-worker. The employees are usually shocked because they had imagined the upper-level management to be a bunch of stuffy, distant slavedrivers who didn't understand them. But once they got to know the head of the company, they felt differently about working for them. Suddenly they felt like they had hope, and that their daily challenges were recognized. They felt understood, and they realized the leadership of the company wasn't so bad after all.

It makes all the difference when you know the one at the top. It changes everything! In the reality show, hopeless employees were transformed into hope-filled employees who were proud to work for their company. In a similar way, the apostle Paul desired nothing more than for believers to know the God of all the universe in a personal way. He wanted them to know Christ—not just know *about* Him, but to really *know* Him. Paul recognized that as the Colossians grew to know Christ, their lives would be transformed from hopeless followers of popular ideas and beliefs to hope-filled followers of Christ. We too have the opportunity to get to know the God of all creation. As we come to know Christ personally our lives can be transformed with a confident hope.

Simply Radiant

When I first met Ellen, I was struck by her radiant smile. At first I didn't notice her cane, but as she gracefully made her way over to meet me I could see that she walked with a slight limp. Ellen told me that she had been diagnosed with spina bifida at birth. Yet she was able to walk, and she was still thriving at 70 years of age. Ellen is literally a walking miracle because back then most children with spina bifida were not expected to live into adulthood. Ellen was able to be the recipient of a very experimental procedure at a young age, which enabled her to walk. When I told Ellen I wanted to write her story she said, "Well, make it all about Jesus, not about me."

Ellen's focus is not on herself; it is on the God who loves and cares for her and continues to shine His light through her. Ellen views her physical limitations from a positive perspective. She recognizes that her challenges offer her an opportunity to reach out and serve other women who have disabilities…and we all have disabilities of some sort. Ellen is a beauty consultant and uses the platform of makeup and outward beauty to talk about the importance of the inner beauty that comes from knowing the Lord. Here's her mission statement:

> *Making a DIFFERENCE in women whose lives have been touched by disability, assisting with their choice for their eternal destiny, one lipstick at a time!*

Ellen realizes that no one is perfect, and our imperfections lead us to a perfect God. It is in Him that we experience strength and joy in life. Ellen's understanding of who God is makes a significant difference in her life. One more thing I must tell you about Ellen is that she loves to pray. She looks to the Lord as her strength day by day, moment by moment, as she visits with Him through prayer. Several times as I was engaged in conversation with Ellen she stopped to say, "Let's go to the Father in prayer about this." Right then and there she prayed. And what a beautiful prayer it was, filled with love and trust and joy in her heavenly Father. Ellen is an example of a woman who lives with a confident hope in the Lord. She lives with a perspective of thankfulness for the opportunity to serve God with her disability. She also lives with a heavenly focus, knowing that this world is not her home and that one day her earthly body will be transformed into a glorious one.

Perspective is everything, and it is a choice. We can view our frustrations and our disappointing circumstances with anger toward God, believing that this life is all we have. Or we can view difficulties from the perspective of "Lord, my eyes are on You. Use me in these circumstances for Your glory. Help me and give me strength along the way." With an eternal perspective we can live with confidence, knowing that this life isn't *it*. We can look forward with confident hope toward heaven and place our confident hope in the God who will care for us here. Ellen is a radiant woman with an eternal perspective. I want to view the world like Ellen!

What's Your Worldview?

One of the big in-vogue words today is *worldview*. The term worldview in some ways comes down to our own personal philosophy in life, meaning the way we view the world in terms of the nature of God, man, morality, knowledge, and even death. For believers in Christ it is important to be aware of other people's worldviews, but what is most important is to know our own personal worldview. Pastor John Piper wrote, "Wimpy worldviews make wimpy Christians. And wimpy Christians won't survive the days ahead."[1] I want to be a confident Christian, not a wimpy one. How about you? Churchleader.net described the importance of our worldview in this way:

> Worldviews act somewhat like eyeglasses or contact lenses. That is, a worldview should provide the correct "prescription" for making sense of the world just as wearing the correct prescription for your eyes brings things into focus.

And, in either example, an incorrect prescription can be dangerous, even life threatening. We are faced with a smorgasbord of worldviews, all of which make claims concerning truth.[2]

It may not be on the top of your to-do list this week, but it is important to consider your personal worldview. What do you believe about God and how He interacts with creation? Have you considered what your purpose is in this world and what God has created you to do? Have you considered where you go from here? Just as the early philosophers began their speculations of life with their view of God, so our journey to significance begins with our view of God. We must seek the truth about Him.

I believe the truth about God is revealed in the Bible. In this matchless book we not only discover the attributes of God, but we also learn how He deals with mankind and what His relationship is with creation. My worldview begins with the Bible. I have a biblical worldview, which means I see the world through the lens of what God revealed in His Word. The Bible is a rock-solid foundation to stand on when it comes to seeking knowledge about life and God. As a young girl I memorized a short verse in the Bible that said, "The grass withers and the flowers fall, but the word of our God stands forever."[3] Philosophies, religions, and cultural beliefs will come and go, but not the precepts of the Bible. It has stood the test of time and will stand as a sure foundation for a worldview throughout all generations.

From the Old Testament we can sense David's biblical worldview:

The law of the Lord *is perfect,*
reviving the soul.
The statutes of the Lord are trustworthy,
making wise the simple.

The precepts of the Lord *are right,*
giving joy to the heart.
The commands of the Lord *are radiant,*
giving light to the eyes.

The fear of the LORD is pure,
enduring forever.
The ordinances of the LORD are sure
and altogether righteous.

They are more precious than gold,
than much pure gold;
they are sweeter than honey,
than honey from the comb.

By them is your servant warned;
in keeping them there is great reward.[4]

If you are seeking wisdom and knowledge; if you hope to find meaning and truth; if you desire to know who God is and how he wants you to live—begin with the Bible. It will light your path and lead you along your journey in life. Paul wrote to Timothy, "All Scripture is God-breathed and is useful for teaching, rebuking, correcting and training in righteousness, so that the man of God may be thoroughly equipped for every good work."[5]

The philosopher Immanuel Kant is quoted as saying, "All the interests of my reason, speculative as well as practical, combine in the three following questions:

1. What can I know?

2. What ought I to do?

3. What may I hope?"[6]

The Bible firmly answers each of those questions. *What can I know?* In the Bible I learn the truth about God and how He relates to His creation. I know I am loved and have a purpose in this world. *What ought I to do?* In the Bible, I learn how God wants me to live, and how He wants me to relate to others. I learn I ought to love Him with all my heart, mind, soul, and strength, and love my neighbor as myself. I learn that if I want to be great in God's kingdom, I must learn to be the servant of all. *What may I hope?* This question is addressed throughout the Bible. I have hope for a glorious future in heaven one day. I have hope that a God who loves me will give me strength and comfort as I walk through the challenges of life. I have hope that He will never leave me alone. I have hope that He knows my needs and hears my prayers.

The Bible answers a lot of questions, doesn't it? So what about you—do you have a biblical worldview? I like how Myrtle Grove Christian School in Wilmington, North Carolina, describes their worldview:

> One of our chief aims at Myrtle Grove Christian School is to instill in students a biblical worldview that is based wholly upon God's Word, the Bible. By worldview, we mean a person's mental framework for understanding the "big picture" of reality, based upon conscious and unconscious assumptions about God, creation, humanity, morality, and purpose.
>
> We believe that the Bible describes the world as it really is. In other words, the Bible answers not only man's religious questions but also the major philosophical questions for which man has always sought answers. The student with a biblical worldview has a system of thought that is unified, logically consistent, and relevant to every area of life. The propositions below provide a brief description of a biblical worldview.
>
> **GOD**
> There is one triune God who is eternally existent in three Persons: Father, Son, and Holy Spirit. He is infinite, personal, sovereign, all powerful, all knowing, and perfect in love, justice and mercy. God is not silent but has revealed Himself to mankind through the Bible, creation, and the person of Jesus Christ.
>
> **CREATION**
> All things were created by God and are sustained by God. Creation consists of a physical realm and a spiritual realm. All of creation was originally good but is now in a fallen state due to the sin of man.

HUMANITY

Humans were created by God in His image and likeness. Consequently, all human life has intrinsic value. At the same time, man lives in a fallen state as a result of sin. Man's sinful condition alienates him from God and renders him unable to worship God properly, live righteously, understand spiritual things, and recognize that all truth in creation reveals the Creator. People can be restored to relationship with God through Jesus Christ.

MORALITY

Morality is based upon the character and nature of God, not upon the consensus of society or culture. It is absolute, not relative. God's moral law is revealed in Scripture, and God commands our compliance with that law.

PURPOSE

God has commanded mankind to have dominion over the earth. Believers are to seek for God's will to be done on earth as it is in heaven and are to be witnesses of Christ to their culture. History is linear, not cyclical, such that humans have only one life to live, and their decisions in that life will affect their eternal destiny.[7]

Now there's a school that knows what they believe! I applaud them for stating it clearly and boldly. Despite the plethora of philosophies rolling around in our culture today, we too can have a clear foundation of what we believe. We must examine everything and hold it up to the light of God's Word to separate God's truth from man's ideas. Just as the Colossians faced the intriguing influences of their culture, so it is tempting to buy into the religious concepts du jour. What's on the menu today?

One of the prevalent schools of thought in Colossae during Paul's day was the early forms of Gnosticism, which emphasized a special, secret knowledge that only a few elite intellectuals possessed. (The Greek work *gnosis* means "to know.") Those who followed the early stages of Gnosticism believed that God was good, but all matter was evil. They didn't believe that Jesus was God, because all created forms are evil, so they declared that Jesus was merely one of a series of emanations descending from God. In their belief system, Jesus must be less than God. They believed in a secret and higher knowledge above the Scriptures. We see similar belief systems in our culture today, yet knowing the God of the Bible can bring clarity to our lives. As you study Colossians, you will grow to know what you believe and be able to walk in a confident knowledge of who you are in Christ.

Paul challenged the Colossians to live lovingly and boldly, and to reflect Christ in what they did and said. I think we could stand to have that reminder as well! All in all, Paul wanted the early Christians to be set apart by their sure faith and unwavering hope in Christ alone. I'm going to make an assumption here, but I'm pretty sure you don't want to lead an empty life based on meaningless philosophies and ideas. I'm guessing you want to live a fulfilled and purposeful life based on truth, God's truth. That's one of the many important lessons we will glean as we journey through this book together. Religious relativism leads us only on an endless search for hope and purpose, but the foundational truths of Christ and His Word lead us to the true source of hope and purpose.

— *Confident Steps* —

ADDITIONAL READING: Psalm 119—The transforming power of God's Word

BATTLE FOR THE TRUTH:

Confidence Defeater—*I have no absolute truth on which to base my life.*

Confidence Builder—Confidence is established when we base our worldview on the sure foundation of the Bible.

CHOICES:

- Seek the truth about God in the Bible, not in current philosophies.
- Examine what you hear and read and hold it up against the light of Scripture.
- Be alert and aware of cultural influences that tend to do battle with your confidence.
- Discover who you are, by getting to know Christ and what He did for you on the cross.
- Live with a heavenly perspective.
- Know your own worldview and what you believe.

DELIBERATE PLAN: Write out your worldview.

Take some time to reflect on your own worldview. Consider the worldview provided in this chapter and write your own statement of belief below.

What I believe about:

God—

Creation—

Humanity—

Morality—

Purpose—

$\mathcal{P}$owerful Prayers You'll Want to Pray

"Be joyful always;
pray continually;
give thanks in all circumstances,
for this is God's will for you in Christ Jesus."

1 THESSALONIANS 5:16-18

"Prayer is not our using of God; it more often puts
us in a position where God can use us."

BILLY GRAHAM

K ind words are like a cup of cool water to a thirsty soul. When someone greets me with an uplifting word and a smile, it renews my spirit and helps me to have a better attitude. What about you? Think about the last time you received a positive boost from a friend or family member. It sets a good tone for the rest of the conversation, doesn't it? The flip side is also true; when someone greets us with a problem or complaint it can be a bit of a downer. Let's be honest, it's not too fun to be greeted with comments such as...

- Where have you been?
- Have you picked up your clothes yet?
- What in the world are you doing?
- What were you thinking?
- You just don't know how hard my day has been.
- Well, it's about time you walked in that door!
- Did you remember to get the…?
- How could you have forgotten?

Not so uplifting, are they? Most likely each of us have been the recipient of comments like those at some point, and yet we must admit that we too may have let a negative greeting slip out of our mouths a time or two as well. Generally speaking, I believe we all desire to bring happiness and joy to others, but sometimes our personal agendas may get ahead of our good intentions. Wouldn't we rather give and receive the following greetings?

- I'm so glad to see you.
- I'm thankful for you.
- You brighten my day.
- How are you feeling?
- I've been praying for you.

Think about the improvement in our relationships if we greeted each other with words like these. We can make a deliberate choice to greet our loved ones with joy instead of burdens. No matter what message we need to get across to a friend or family member, we can always start on a positive note. That's what Paul did. He had a deep concern about the growing heresy in the Colossian church, but he chose to start out his letter with a kind, uplifting greeting, instead of saying, "Dear church at Colossae, what in the world are you thinking?" Kindness always draws more attention than anger, and if we want to make an impact or see true change, we must first build up, not tear down.

Here's how Paul started out his letter:

COLOSSIANS 1:1-2

Paul, an apostle of Christ Jesus by the will of God,
* and Timothy our brother,*
To the holy and faithful brothers in Christ at Colosse:
* Grace and peace to you from God our Father.*

It is important to note that Paul wrote this letter while he was under house arrest and in chains in Rome for preaching the gospel. Yes, Mr. Sunshine was in chains. Note to self: If I am waiting for my life to get better in order to be kind and uplifting to others, then I'd better stop waiting. Paul was constantly encouraging and inspiring others while he was a prisoner. We have no excuses. No more waiting! We need to build up others in the midst of our not-so-perfect lives. Let's not waste any more time being negative—rather, let's reach out and be proactive with kind and thoughtful words for others.

Notice that Paul called himself an "apostle," which means one who is chosen and sent by God. He often started off letters with the identification of himself as an apostle to establish his authority and his credibility. He also included the words "by the will of God" to remind the recipients that it wasn't his own ambition or personal aspirations that made him an apostle, it was God's plan. Since Paul wasn't one of the original 12 disciples, he offered his credentials so there wouldn't be any doubt about his authority to address the church on matters of doctrine.

Paul described the Colossians as holy and faithful. I'm sure the Colossians were sitting a little taller as they heard the opening greeting from Paul. I also think they probably leaned in a little closer to hear what this man of God had to say to them, since after all they were "holy and faithful" brothers and sisters in Christ. By calling them holy, Paul didn't mean that they were perfect people. *Holy* is used to describe a person or object that is set apart, consecrated to God. Because of their faith in Christ, they were set apart as God's people. *Faithful* indicates that they were believers, trusting in Christ for their salvation.

Paul's greeting is not just for the Colossians. It can describe those of us who have placed our faith in Christ and follow Him. Do you see yourself as holy and faithful? It's hard to think of ourselves in those terms, especially when we have just yelled at the kids or gotten angry at a co-worker. Yet as believers in Christ, we are His beloved people. It's not that we are gleaming, righteous, or deserving in and of ourselves, but through Christ's death on the cross we are made holy in Him. As believers, trusting in Him, we are set apart as His own beloved people. What a privilege and an honor to be consecrated to Him—set apart to serve Him! Take a moment right now to thank the Father for what Christ did on the cross and for allowing you to have the privilege to be one of His holy and faithful people.

Thanks-Filled Prayers

It's one thing to pray for another person, but it is entirely a different thing to thank God for a person. When we sincerely thank God for people, it changes the way we look at them. We begin to focus on their good qualities, and we also recognize that God has put them in our lives for a purpose. Yes, even the difficult people! I'm sure Paul was able to start out his letter with such an uplifting greeting because he was actively thanking God for the Colossians and for the good qualities they exhibited. He didn't focus on what was wrong with them, but rather gave attention to what was right about them. A lesson we could all use!

Here's how Paul let the Colossians know the way he felt about them:

COLOSSIANS 1:3-8

We always thank God, the Father of our Lord Jesus Christ, when we pray for you, because we have heard of your faith in Christ Jesus and of the love you have for all the saints—the faith and love that spring from the hope that is stored up for you in heaven and that you have already heard about in the word of truth, the gospel that has come to you. All over the world this gospel is bearing fruit and growing, just as it has been doing among you since the day you heard it and understood God's grace in all its truth. You learned it from Epaphras, our dear fellow servant, who is a faithful minister of Christ on our behalf, and who also told us of your love in the Spirit.

It may be tempting to skip over the significance of Paul's thankful prayers for the Colossians, since he often used this kind of greeting in his letters. I don't believe Paul was just saying he thanked God for them as a generic, blanket greeting. It seems evident that he was sincerely thankful for his fellow believers at Colossae. Notice he specifically told them the qualities for which he was thankful—their faith and love. Paul wanted his brothers and sisters in Christ to know that he was not only thankful for their faith in Christ Jesus, but he was glad to see their faith growing and bearing fruit in their lives. One of the ways their faith was bearing fruit was through their love toward each other. Paul commended the Colossians for their love they had for all the saints. What a beautiful evidence of God's Spirit at work in the body of Christ! If we exhibit a sincere love for all of our fellow sisters in Christ, God is glorified and people are drawn to Christ.

When I see the word "all" it says to me that no one was left out. "All" means embracing those who are similar to you as well as those who are different from you. It means looking past racial or denominational lines. If we love *all* the saints in Christ Jesus, then we are to love the ones who maybe don't dress the same way we would dress. It means we love the ones who aren't in the popular crowd. When we love *all*, we love the ones who have physical handicaps and the ones who aren't able to give as much money to the church budget. As believers in Christ, we are *all* unworthy recipients of His grace and love. I like the word "all." We are never so beautiful as when we overflow with a love for *all* God's people and we don't pick and choose.

> *Father, renew in us a love for all Your people. Fill us with a sincere love that looks past barriers and reaches out to touch those who seem different than us. Father, may Your love be so overwhelmingly evident in our lives that all believers would feel drawn into a deeper relationship with You.*

Faith and love go hand in hand. When we take a step of faith, believing in the Lord Jesus, God's Spirit begins to do a transforming work in our lives. The God of love begins to fill us with His love and that love overflows to those around us. God's love changes us. When we recognize that we are holy and dearly loved by God, we in turn desire to love others. How easily we forget the sincere love of the Father toward us! We become distracted with the desire to be loved and adored by people, and often we fail to remember that we are abundantly loved by our heavenly Father. When we place our faith in Christ Jesus, the Bible says we are a part of His family; we are one of His children. The Bible also reminds us that as a father has compassion on his children, so the Lord has compassion on those who fear Him.[1] He is slow to anger and abounding in love. Earthly fathers may let us down, but nothing can separate us from our heavenly Father's love.

Notice how Paul said the Colossians' faith and love *spring* (in other words, have arisen) from the hope stored up for them in heaven. Paul continually pointed believers to the hope of glory. When our minds are focused on the hope we have beyond this world, it makes us realize how silly or trivial most worries and arguments are in our lives. When we live with the hope of heaven, we live with the joy of anticipation. We are all a little more loving toward others when we don't get bent out of shape over temporal things that don't matter. Let us live with our hearts toward heaven, and allow our faith and love to spring from our eternal perspective.

Radiant Prayer Warrior

As the mother of three young girls, Becky wouldn't have much time for prayer, you would think, but she makes time throughout her busy day. Prayer is a priority to Becky. I know, because she prays for me continually. Becky keeps a copy of my speaking and writing schedule, and she always leaves me a message while I am speaking, telling me how she is praying for me. Honestly, I find it incredible that every time she prays for me, she knows just how to pray. She seems to know exactly what I need for the specific group to whom I am speaking. Only someone in tune with God's Spirit could do such a thing.

Becky is a rich blessing to my life because of the gift she gives me through her prayers. The way we first met each other was a huge

God-thing. A number of years ago I was on a girlfriends' weekend away with some of my high-school buddies, and Becky was on a personal 24-hour retreat away from the kids (a gift from her husband). We were all staying at a bed and breakfast in McKinney, Texas. I had to leave before breakfast (bummer—B and B breakfasts are the best) in order to meet some workmen at my house, so my three high-school friends invited Becky to join them at their table for breakfast. As they visited with her they began to realize she had quite a bit in common with me. Our husbands were in the same business, we both had two blond-haired daughters (this was before number three came along for Becky), and we both have long blond hair. One of my friends said, "Well, if you write books, then we are going to start calling you Karol."

It was then that Becky said, "Wait a minute—Karol who?" When they told Becky about me, Becky was shocked. She had just been upstairs prayerfully reading over her journal and reflecting on some quotes from my book *The Power of a Positive Mom*, which she had bought and read years ago. Well, you can imagine my friends got right on the phone and told me to get back to McKinney as soon as I could. Becky and I have been heart sisters ever since that day. Becky walks with Jesus step by step as she prays and seeks His direction. She is a group leader in a large Bible study in Dallas, and serves the Lord with gladness in a variety of different areas. I'm thankful for a confident prayer warrior like Becky, who shines brightly in her home and community for Christ.

The Beauty of Prayer

Paul was a prayer warrior. As we consider all the great men and women of faith throughout the ages, we see a common thread—they were prayer warriors. They did diligent battle on their knees before they set out to achieve great things for the kingdom. Listen to the voices of faithful men and women throughout the ages as they join in the chorus acknowledging the beautiful discipline of prayer.

- "He who has learned to pray has learned the greatest secret of a holy and happy life."—William Law

- "Sometimes we think we are too busy to pray. That is a great mistake, for praying is a saving of time."
  —C.H. Spurgeon
- "Of all things, guard against neglecting God in the secret place of prayer."—William Wilberforce
- "Prayer is a strong wall and fortress of the church; it is a godly Christian's weapon."—Martin Luther
- "Prayer does not fit us for the greater work; prayer is the greater work."—Oswald Chambers
- "There is no way that Christians, in a private capacity, can do so much to promote the work of God and advance the kingdom of Christ as by prayer."
  —Jonathan Edwards
- "When a Christian shuns fellowship with other Christians, the devil smiles. When he stops studying the Bible, the devil laughs. When he stops praying, the devils shouts for joy."—Corrie ten Boom
- "Rich is the person who has a praying friend."
  —Janice Hughes

I must stop and share a personal story with you that happened as I was writing this chapter. You see, as I read the last quote by Janice Hughes in the lineup of quotes above, I stopped typing and asked the Lord to give me someone that would pray specifically for me while I was writing this chapter. I poured out my heart to the Lord on this matter, knowing that I needed God's help and guidance right then and there, as I had experienced several interruptions that morning and was having trouble focusing on what to write. Several minutes later my cell phone rang, displaying a long-distance number I didn't recognize. Normally I don't answer the phone when I am writing, but I felt as though I maybe should get this call just in case it might be an emergency or something.

When I answered, a dear sweet voice on the other end said, "Oh

Karol, I didn't think you would pick up. I just wanted to leave you a message and let you know I am praying for you. This is Debbie Williams, and just a moment ago the Lord prompted me to pray for you. Since I have you on the line, is there anything I can pray about?" Now I want you to know that I hadn't talked to Debbie in a long time. She is a fellow author who has written several books specifically on (you guessed it) prayer![2] She loves the Lord and is a devoted woman of prayer. Do you have chills yet?

Immediately I shared with Debbie that I had just asked God for someone to pray for me concerning the writing of this chapter. She was thrilled to be a part of God's plan, and she was glad that she had followed God's prompting and called me. If anyone can understand the pressure of writing, it is a fellow author, so she knew exactly how to pray for me. She offered up a wonderful and heartfelt prayer for this book and for God's direction as I wrote. She then got off the phone quickly, saying she didn't want to take up any more of my writing time, although she agreed to continue to pray for this book.

One of my friends uses the term "God bumps" instead of goose bumps to refer to the tingly feeling you get when you see God work in significant ways in your life. I have God bumps as I write this! My friends, I want you to know, God wants us to pray. He hears our prayers, and He answers them. We may not see the answer as quickly and obviously as I saw it today. God may not give us exactly what we ask for, but He hears our prayers. We can trust His sovereignty to know what is best for our lives. I am overwhelmed by the way God loves us and so tenderly cares about the details of our lives. He is not distant; He is near. When we pray and watch God work, it increases our faith in our loving heavenly Father.

A Powerful Prayer

Janice Hughes is right: "Rich is the person who has a praying friend." Yes, I am a spiritually rich person due to friends like Debbie and Becky. The Colossian church was also rich because they had a praying friend like Paul. Wouldn't we all love to have the apostle Paul as our prayer warrior? Here we catch a glimpse of the powerful prayers he prayed:

COLOSSIANS 1:9-11

For this reason, since the day we heard about you, we have not stopped praying for you and asking God to fill you with the knowledge of his will through all spiritual wisdom and understanding. And we pray this in order that you may live a life worthy of the Lord and may please him in every way: bearing fruit in every good work, growing in the knowledge of God, being strengthened with all power according to his glorious might so that you may have great endurance and patience...

Paul wanted all the best for the Colossian believers. He wanted them to be filled with the knowledge of God's will through spiritual wisdom and understanding. Spiritual wisdom and understanding looks different than the world's wisdom and understanding. God doesn't want us to aimlessly wander through this world. He wants us to know how to act and how to live according to His will. We can walk confidently when we know we are walking on the foundation of His will. But how do we know His will? We begin to know it when we turn from thinking like the world thinks and instead focus on what God says. The Bible is our source to know what He says. He uses godly people and wise counsel in our lives as well, but we must always consider their words in accordance with His Word.

Paul prays that the Colossians would live a life worthy of the Lord and please Him in every way. As Christians we must live in a manner consistent with our faith in Christ. If we say we follow Christ, then we need to walk in obedience to Him. Jesus said, "If you obey my commands, you will remain in my love...I have told you this so that my joy may be in you and that your joy may be complete."[3] There is great joy as we live a life that pleases Him. It is tempting to think that living a life to please ourselves brings us joy, but true and lasting joy comes when we walk in God's ways. Paul wanted the best for the Colossians when he prayed that they would please God in every way. We are joyful women when we live a life that pleases God.

Now another aspect we know about God's will is that He intends for us as Christians to be fruitful. Paul prayed for the Colossians to be "fruitful in every good work." Picture the beauty in that one phrase. I want my good work to be fruitful. I don't want to just labor in vain. Are you with me here? Fruitful Christians make a positive difference in this world as their efforts flourish and grow and bring joy to others. Throughout the Bible we find references to spiritual fruit. Jesus said when we abide in Him we bear much fruit.[4] Paul wrote that the fruit of God's Spirit is love, joy, peace, patience, kindness, goodness, faithfulness, gentleness, and self-control.[5] Now those are radiant qualities!

> *Yes, Lord—allow us to bear fruit in every good work and grow in the knowledge of You!*

Amazing Inheritance

When Sergey Sudev was told that he had inherited 950 million euros from a distant uncle, he thought it was a joke, but he was soon laughing all the way to the bank. Sergey had not seen his uncle, who lived in Germany, for ten years, but apparently he had made an impression, because it was then that the uncle wrote him into his will. As a student in journalism Sergey had no idea he had the possibility to inherit a fortune, but now he has become one of the richest men in Moldova, where the average monthly salary is around 270 euros. Although he could sit back and bask in his wealth, Sudev intends to complete his journalism studies. Unfortunately his studying is now continually interrupted by people asking for loans.

Can you imagine being catapulted from poverty into becoming one of the wealthiest people in your country overnight? I'm sure it has taken Sergey some time to get used to the fact that his life will never be the same. The Bible says that we too have received a great inheritance—only not financially, but rather, spiritually. Before we knew Christ we were bankrupt. We owed a debt we could not pay in the form of our own sin and disobedience to God. We can't pay off our own sin debt, only Christ can. Perhaps you are thinking to yourself, *Well, I haven't sinned so much. I'm a pretty good person. Surely I can pay my sin debt off by being good.* The Bible says all have sinned and come short of God's glory.[6] The Bible also says that the wages of sin is death, but the free gift of God is eternal life through Jesus Christ our Lord.[7]

We don't deserve to receive an inheritance to pay off our sin debt, yet God freely gives it to all who receive Christ through faith. Just as Sergey received his inheritance when he opened the door and accepted it, so we receive our inheritance when we accept Christ, by trusting in Him.[8] As Paul prayed for his fellow believers he also prayed that they would joyfully give thanks to God because of the inheritance they had received. Here's how he put it:

COLOSSIANS 1:12

...and joyfully giving thanks to the Father, who has qualified you to share in the inheritance of the saints in the kingdom of light.

Now if I had just received an incredible inheritance like Sergey's, I wouldn't just stuff it in my pocket and silently walk away with a frown. No, if it were me, I'd be singing and dancing and smiling and shouting and sharing the good news! I'd live with a joyful and thankful heart. I'd be grateful every day for what I had received. Wait a minute—why don't we as Christians live like that? Why don't we joyfully give thanks each day to the Father for what He has done for us? I can understand why Paul prayed these words for the Colossians. We need those good words too. How soon we forget what God has done for us. We share in the inheritance of the saints in the kingdom of light. Ponder that one truth for a moment, then joyfully give thanks to the Father. Let's ask the Lord to help us live each day with the joy of our inheritance.

Rescued!

Our nation recently experienced one of the worst oil disasters in history, the BP oil crisis in the Gulf of Mexico. One of the many unfortunate victims in this tragedy is the wildlife. We've seen many sad pictures on the evening news of pelicans covered in oil and the valiant effort to clean them up. Rescue workers have been working tirelessly to take in the pelicans, scrub them up, and send them off into a safe environment. The before and after pictures show the dramatic difference of a pelican covered in oil and then transformed into a clean bird once again. In fact, I'm pretty sure those birds have never been so clean in all their lives.

The pelicans couldn't clean themselves up. They were in a hopeless situation and needed to be rescued. The dark oil that covered their feathers and threatened their lives is like the darkness of sin that covered our lives. We too needed to be rescued—from the dominion of darkness. Here's how Paul put it:

COLOSSIANS 1:13-14

He has rescued us from the dominion of darkness and brought us into the kingdom of the Son he loves, in whom we have redemption, the forgiveness of sins.

The term *rescue* actually means "to draw to oneself" or "to deliver." God lovingly drew us to Himself, saving us from the power of darkness and transferring us to the kingdom of His beloved Son. Redemption means we were paid for, bought, with the price of Christ's blood. We are forgiven, pardoned—the penalty of our sin is removed. To be clear, not the consequence of sin, but the penalty is gone.

Dear sister in Christ, do you recognize the beautiful transformation God has created in our lives through Christ? When I read this passage, I can't help but be overwhelmed with the truth of God's kindness toward us. We are rescued, redeemed, and forgiven. What confidence we can have because of this truth! What overflowing joy! He has done it! God has rescued us from the muck and enslaving power of sin. He has cleaned us up and set us free. It doesn't mean we will never sin again, but the power of sin has no control over us as believers in Christ.

In this chapter, we have gleaned great truths from the prayers Paul prayed. It is my hope that each of us has been challenged and inspired not only to pray more fervently, but also to recognize the confidence we can have in coming to God as His rescued and redeemed children. I want to close with a quote from Andrew Murray that pulls together much of what we have learned in this chapter: "Each time, before you intercede, be quiet first, and worship God in His glory. Think of what He can do, and how He delights to hear the prayers of His redeemed people. Think of your place and privilege in Christ, and expect great things!"

Confident Steps

ADDITIONAL READING: John 17—Jesus prays for His followers

BATTLE FOR THE TRUTH:

Confidence Defeater—*I'm not good enough for God to answer my prayers.*

Confidence Builder—As believers, we can pray with confidence when we recognize our heavenly Father's love and grace toward us.

CHOICES:

- Greet people with kindness, no matter what your life is like.
- Actively and consistently thank God for the people in your life.
- Grow in the knowledge of God's will by studying His Word.
- Ask God to allow your good work to be fruitful.
- Joyfully thank God for being allowed to share in the inheritance of the saints in the kingdom of light.
- Recognize you are rescued, redeemed, and forgiven.

DELIBERATE PLAN: Offer to be a prayer warrior for a friend.

Just as Paul diligently prayed for the early church, so we too can be a faithful warrior for a friend. Ask the Lord to lead you to one friend for whom you will consistently pray. Contact the person and ask them if they have any specific prayer needs. Use Paul's prayer as a pattern for prayers.

Wonderful and faithful Father, I pray that you would fill _____ with the knowledge of Your will through all spiritual wisdom and understanding. And Father, I pray that _____ may live a life worthy of You and that she (he) may please You in every way: bearing fruit in every good work, growing in Your knowledge. Please help _____ to be strengthened with all power according to Your glorious might so that she (he) may have great endurance and patience. I joyfully give thanks to You, because You have qualified us as Your followers to share in the inheritance of the saints in the kingdom of light.

PART TWO

Grow in Christ

"I am the vine; you are the branches.
If a man remains in me and I in him,
he will bear much fruit;
apart from me you can do nothing."

JOHN 15:5

"If I have observed anything by experience it is this:
a man may take the measure of his growth and
decay in grace according to his thoughts and
meditations upon the person of Christ and the
glory of Christ's kingdom and of his love."

JOHN OWEN

CHAPTER THREE

The Joy of Knowing Him

"In the beginning was the Word,
and the Word was with God,
and the Word was God.
He was with God in the beginning.
Through him all things were made;
without him nothing was made that has been made."

JOHN 1:1-3

"It is by looking at Jesus that we discover who God is.
He is the image of God, the invisible one.
Nobody has ever seen God,
but in Jesus he has come near to us and become one of us."

N.T. WRIGHT

When I was a little girl I used to watch old, scary movies on television. Now "scary" back then was very different from "scary" today. Bloody chainsaw massacres were not around. No, I watched the black-and-white, almost laughable films like *Frankenstein Meets the Wolfman* or *The Mummy Lives*. One movie I remember watching was a thriller based on a book by H.G. Wells called *The Invisible Man*. It's all about a scientist who figures out a way to make himself invisible, and he goes around scaring people (at least that's how I remember the movie). Imagine if someone could really be invisible. In my little-girl imagination I thought that there actually could be an invisible man. I was afraid to go to bed for weeks, thinking an invisible person could be in my room. Finally my parents helped me understand that it was just a story and it was scientifically impossible for there to be a real, true invisible man. Funny, the things that freak us out as little kids!

The invisible man doesn't exist, but the invisible God does. And thankfully He is not trying to scare us. Throughout the Bible we see references made to the invisible God. Paul wrote to Timothy, "Now to the King eternal, immortal, invisible, the only God, be honor and glory for ever and ever."[1] Jesus said, "God is spirit, and his worshipers must worship in spirit and in truth."[2] In the Gospel of John we read, "The law was given through Moses, but God's unfailing love and faithfulness came through Jesus Christ. No one has ever seen God. But the one and only Son is himself God and is near to the Father's heart. He has revealed God to us."[3]

It is difficult to even begin to get a picture in mind of the greatness and vastness of God. The beautiful truth is that although we cannot see God, we can see what He looks like as we look at Jesus. We may struggle in our human minds to understand the image of God, but Jesus is God with skin on. He is the perfect representation of the invisible God. As Paul continued his letter to the Colossians he wanted to turn the spotlight onto Christ. Who is Jesus really? He is not an angel, He is not just another good guy—He is the image of God because He is God. Here's how Paul put it:

COLOSSIANS 1:15-20

He (Christ) is the image of the invisible God, the firstborn over all creation. For by him all things were created: things in heaven and on earth, visible and invisible, whether thrones or powers or rulers or authorities; all things were created by him and for him. He is before all things, and in him all things hold together. And he is the head of the body, the church; he is the beginning and the firstborn from among the dead, so that in everything he might have the supremacy. For God was pleased to have all his fullness dwell in him, and through him to

> *reconcile to himself all things, whether things on earth or things in heaven, by making peace through his blood, shed on the cross.*

What a powerful description of Christ! If you have ever wanted to understand who Jesus Christ is and what He has done, you find it clearly and precisely right here in this passage. This is considered one of the central passages in Scripture that describe Christ. This short section is overflowing with such treasures of truth that I dare say several volumes of books could be written just on this passage. It is Christology at its finest. In order for us to discover who we are in Christ, we must first know who He is. Our journey to confidence begins with Him.

Photograph of God

Whenever someone sees a picture of me with one of my daughters they will say to me, "Oh, she looks exactly like you. She is the spitting image of you." I especially love it when someone says we look like sisters. Yes, that person becomes my new best friend! But if you look at a picture of me with my daughters, the only exact image of me is actually the picture of *me*, not my daughters. Now if cameras had been invented back in Paul's day, his words would have been more like, "Jesus is the photograph of God." The word for "image" in the original Greek is *eikon*, meaning likeness, representation, or statue. We get the term *icon* from this word. In classical Greek it referred to a dye or stamp, but in the New Testament times it meant a precise copy or exact replica. In today's terms, we would say photocopy or photograph. It's as if you could hold your camera up to take a picture of the invisible God, and the image that is produced in the picture is Jesus.

Why is this important? Why does it matter that Jesus was the image of the invisible God? Because misconceptions about Christ flourish. They did back when Paul wrote this letter and they still do today. As followers of Christ we must know what we believe about Him, beginning with the fact that He is God in the flesh. The philosophical pundits of Paul's day (the early Gnostics) said Jesus could not have been God, because they believed that all matter or fleshly material was evil. They also believed that anything of the spirit was good. If God was good (because He is a spirit), then He would not have become flesh, which is evil. Because of their philosophy there was no way that a good God could dwell in an evil capacity or human body. The Gnostics speculated that Jesus therefore must have been a good angel or an emanation, not man, not God. It was Paul's intention to clear up the Colossians' confusion.

God doesn't want us to be confused about Christ. Jesus Christ's deity is central to our Christian foundation and beliefs. If you believe that Jesus was just a nice man or a wise prophet or a good angel, then you are missing the very essence of Christianity. Paul made it clear that Jesus was all man and all God. There is no one else who fits that description. Christ is the one and only God in human form. Immanuel, God with us, sent to this world to offer His life for us.

In Colossians we see one of the strongest statements in all of Scripture as to the divine nature of Christ. He is supreme over all creation and over all spiritual beings. He is the one who created us and sustains us. Later in Colossians Paul talks about how we are hidden in Christ. Now I don't know about you, but if I am going to be hidden in someone's arms, I want to be able to know him and trust him. As this passage paints a true picture of Jesus in vibrant color, I see the power and the beauty of the One in whom I have placed my trust. I know I can safely and confidently place my life in His loving arms. Yes, when I recognize the truths Paul proclaimed, I want to be hidden in Jesus. Here's what I learn about Christ in this passage:

- He is the visible image of the invisible God.
- He is the firstborn (supreme) over all creation.
- By Him all things were created.
- He existed before everything else began.
- He holds all creation together.
- He is the Head of the church.
- He is the firstborn of all who will rise from the dead.
- In everything He has the supremacy—He is supreme over all, the first in everything.

- All God's fullness dwells in Him and through Him.
- God reconciled all things through Christ, by making peace through His blood shed on the cross.

> *Praise You, Father, Son, and Holy Spirit, God three in One. There is no other. You are the God of all creation, the beginning and the end. Loving, merciful, all-wise God, all glory and honor belong to You. You are before all things, and by You all things exist. Thank You, God, for caring about me. I am honored to be called Your daughter. Glorious God, thank You for letting me know You through Your Son Jesus. Holy, Holy, Holy, Lord God Almighty, You are the One who was and is and is to come.*

It's Personal

What do we do with the facts about Jesus? Do we just store them in our brains as important knowledge or are they truths that transform our lives? Paul wasn't just listing these facts simply for the Colossians' intellectual advantage, He wanted them to live and move and breathe Christ. It is one thing to look at a portrait of Jesus; it is another to know Him, the artist of all creation, personally. What a wonderful privilege we have to embrace Him with our heart, mind, and soul. Let's choose to take Jesus Christ personally as we look at the truths listed in this passage and consider how they affect our lives.

Image of the invisible God. God lovingly revealed Himself to mankind through Jesus. God in His holiness could have chosen to remain distant and obscure, invisible, and untouchable. Once again I think of the invisible man. He enjoyed his anonymity, yet when he fell in love he wanted his beloved to know who he was and where he was, so he put on a trench coat and hat and wrapped cloth bandages around his skin. As believers in Christ, we are God's beloved and precious ones. He wanted us to know what He was like, so in His kindness He came in human form. How wonderful to think that the God of all creation, the High King of heaven, chose to reach out and pursue us, to show us Himself in the form of Jesus—God with skin on.

What did Jesus look like here on earth? Love. Forgiving, grace-filled, enduring love. He reached out to the unlovely, the hurting, and the ones who felt alone. He looked into their hearts. He didn't look at their status, their accomplishments, their fame or power. He saw people for who they really were on the inside. Jesus was powerful, yet gentle. Wise and understanding. He served, He helped, He gave, He encouraged, He admonished, and He spoke the truth in love. That's a true reflection of what God looks like.

Firstborn over all creation. The term *firstborn* actually refers to the one who is the highest-ranking in authority, the chief, the heir with the greatest privilege and responsibility. First-century Jews knew exactly what it meant in the context of their own families. They honored the firstborn with the highest rights (double inheritance) and privileged position. They had a deep sense of respect for the firstborn and must have understood exactly what Paul meant by ascribing to Jesus the respected position of firstborn over all creation. Paul was declaring Jesus as the supreme and highest authority. He is above all creation, although He Himself was not created, for He always existed. Jesus was not one of many gods. He was and is chief ruler over all He created.

He is in authority over us as His creation. He does not pridefully lord His pre-eminent rank over us, but rather lovingly and humbly came and laid down His life for us. We can choose to trust His leading and acknowledge His supremacy, or we can buck against Him, rebel, and do things our way. Personally, I would much rather fall into His powerful and loving arms through obedience to Him. We are in good hands when we are in His hands. He is in authority over all creation, and He is sovereign over all things. All creation answers to Jesus. When things go differently than we planned or our life circumstances turn upside down, there is a strength and peace we can experience in knowing that all creation answers to the One who holds us in His hands. He is in control, and He is not surprised by what has happened, and He will see us through.

By Him all things were created. Jesus created all things in heaven and on earth, visible and invisible, whether thrones or powers or rulers or authorities. Well, I guess Paul covered everything! For the Gnostics of Paul's day, this blew their whole theory of Jesus. Remember, the Gnostics believed that all matter was bad and God was good. They believed that God didn't create matter, and that God couldn't be linked to it. Obviously the argument of origins and creation is nothing new. It has been discussed and debated throughout the generations, but Paul makes one thing perfectly clear—all things were created by God. (The Trinity—Father, Son, and Spirit. Notice the plural pronouns we read in the creation account found in Genesis, "Then God said, 'Let us make man in our image, in our likeness.'"[4])

He is *the* creator, and He is *our* creator. He created us in His likeness. We are not His exact likeness or image (only Christ is the exact image of God), but we reflect His character in our being. Our ability to create, to connect, to love, to show patience, to give kindness, to offer forgiveness all reflect His nature. Knowing God created us in His likeness gives us a sense of worth and purpose. God placed His nature in you and in me. He created us, and He does not make mistakes. Do not listen to that voice that whispers in your ear, "You are worthless. There is no purpose for your life." These are lies from the enemy. You are a creation of God almighty. He knew exactly what He was doing when He created you. Listen to His voice saying, "My beloved daughter, I knew you in your mother's womb. You didn't just happen. I formed you and I created you and I have a purpose for your life."

Confidence grows on the foundation of Christ—knowing who He is and that He created you and redeemed you. My friend, never forget that you were created by Him. He knows your name. He knows your challenges. He understands your pain. He loves you as His precious creation. Take time each day to thank the Lord for creating you. I'm not asking you to say it in a prideful way: "Well, isn't the world lucky to have me?" Rather, I'm encouraging you to pray in a humble way, "Thank You, Lord, that You created me, and that all I am comes from You. Thank You that You have a purpose for me, and You have equipped me exactly for that purpose." Do you see how that prayer takes away pride yet builds confidence, a God-confidence? I challenge you to thank God daily for the way He created you, because Satan would love for you to *forget* each day that you are God's creation, formed by His loving hands.

He existed before everything else began. How powerful is your picture of Jesus? Do you see Him as a mild-mannered man who walked this earth, as you recall from the sweet little Sunday-school pictures hanging on the wall? Or do you recognize that He is everlasting, the almighty God, the Alpha and the Omega, the great I AM? From eternity to eternity, there is no beginning or end to Christ. He is the everlasting One, the Lord of all, who always was and always is and always will be.

It's impossible to wrap our finite brains around the concept of eternity, isn't it? As a former math teacher, I used to use a number line to represent how numbers go on forever and ever in both directions. Jesus' existence is infinite in both directions, as we see represented in the number line. Actually He is infinite in all directions, time and space included. On the other hand, our existence is like a ray, which is a line with a starting point that goes on in one direction. We were created, and we will go on to spend eternity either with God or without Him. When our hope is placed in the everlasting One, we can rejoice in knowing that one day we will be with Him in eternity.

How amazing to think that the everlasting God cares about my life and yours. He wants us to spend eternity with Him, and that's why He sent Jesus to die on the cross. The gift of God is eternal life through faith in Jesus. The Bible reminds us, "From everlasting to everlasting the LORD's love is with those who fear him." Just as God has no time limits, His love has no limits for those who believe. As high as the heavens are above the earth, so great is His love toward those who fear Him. As far as the east is from the west, so far has He removed our transgressions from us.[5]

In examining the infinitude or limitlessness of God, A.W. Tozer wrote, "At the contemplation and utterance of His majesty all eloquence is rightly dumb, all mental effort is feeble. For God is greater than mind itself."[6] Tozer went on to talk about the limitless love of the Father. "His love is something He is, and because He is infinite that love can enfold the whole created world in itself and have room for ten thousand times ten thousand worlds beside."[7] Oh, the greatness of the everlasting God! His loving-kindness knows no bounds. Rejoice in His everlasting love!

He holds all creation together. In the physical universe we observe the beauty of His handiwork and realize that God holds all things together, from the vast galaxies in the universe to the microscopic DNA in our bodies. We must care for His creation and not abuse it whether it is our environment or our bodies. As we recognize Jesus as both Creator and Sustainer of all creation, we must also understand that nothing happens apart from Him. The healthy balance is that we respect creation because we love the Creator, but we also recognize that we don't hold creation's future in our hands—God does.

We cannot ignore the perfect balance that exists upon and within our own planet, and we must recognize that Jesus certainly holds all things together. Hank Hanegraaff, president of Christian Research Institute International, puts it this way:

> From the temperatures to the tides and the tap water, and myriad other characteristics that we so easily take for granted, the earth is an unparalleled planetary masterpiece. Like Handel's *Messiah* or da Vinci's *Last Supper*, it should never be carelessly pawned off as the result of blind evolutionary processes.[8]

Knowing the One who holds all things together gives us great comfort on many fronts. I may not know what is around the corner or what tomorrow holds, but I do know who holds tomorrow. He is our Keeper and our Sustainer. I'm reminded of the psalmist's words:

> *I lift up my eyes to the hills—*
> *where does my help come from?*
> *My help comes from the LORD,*
> *the Maker of heaven and earth.*

He will not let your foot slip—
    he who watches over you will not slumber;
indeed, he who watches over Israel
    will neither slumber nor sleep.
The LORD *watches over you—*
    the LORD *is your shade at your right hand;*
the sun will not harm you by day,
    nor the moon by night.
The LORD *will keep you from all harm—*
    he will watch over your life;
the LORD *will watch over your coming and going*
    both now and forevermore.[9]

As the Creator and Artist of life, He can take the broken pieces of our lives and put them together to form a beautiful mosaic. He holds our lives together when we are struggling to make sense out of our disappointments. He holds our lives together when our family or our job or our finances are falling apart. My friend, look to Him for peace and strength as you go through the storms of life. He is able to hold you together when you feel like you can't go on. Seek His face; ask for His comfort and direction. Fall into the arms of the One who is your Keeper, your Sustainer, your Creator.

He Held Her Life Together

Throughout the pain and difficulties of her life, Leslie O'Hare learned that it was God who held her life together and had a plan all along the way. Here's a glimpse into her life as she tells her story:

Have you ever experienced the "I Got It Moment"? Some may call it a life lesson, but I prefer to call it the "I Got It Moment." Because once you get it, the fact that God loves you and can pull together the pieces of your life, you learn from it and it sticks with you forever. We should look at every day of our life as a new day to become more educated than the day before. Well, I truly "got it" about one year ago. Keep in mind I thought I always had it. Until I went through about twenty years of my life searching and hoping to fulfill a long passion and dream of becoming a successful television talk show host and businesswoman. I wanted to build my own media empire. You may say, "Wow, it took you twenty years to get it?" Yes, twenty years, but the most important part is that I got it.

I didn't quite understand why I had a father that chose not to have anything to do with me, but chose to have everything to do with his children with his current wife. In my early twenties my mother and I moved to New York City in order for me to pursue my acting career on "The Cosby Show" as well as modeling. I didn't understand why when it appeared things were going so great in my career, my mother became terribly ill. I had to become her mother and with God's help to nurse her back to health. I didn't understand why I had to make the decision to give up my hopes and dreams to now take on the role of a parent taking care of my mother. I didn't understand why during those years of taking care of my mother we had it so hard financially, literally living from paycheck to paycheck to make ends meet. Every bill in the house was on me at such an early age. Eventually my mother began to get better and God gave her strength to live her life, still in some pain, but alive and now able to take care of herself.

I didn't understand why my relationship with my mother had to go sour when I chose to get married. She struggled to understand that I needed to leave the nest in order to grow and learn more about who God made me to be. I didn't understand why God gave me awesome positions in corporate America after I gave up my acting career, but along the way I encountered lots of jealousy and bitterness from my women counterparts because of my strong work ethic, which allowed me to constantly get promoted along the way.

You see, I always felt during those trials and tribulations that

I took one step forward and also took fifty steps backward. Every time I would try to pick myself up and start all over again to pursue my God-given talent something else would come my way to just knock me right back down. However, I finally had my "I Got It Moment"…During those times of feeling as though I was in a darkroom like a photographer who's developing photos, I realized that Christ was developing, educating, strengthening, and empowering me to get ready for such a time as this. Christ was preparing me for a new season of my life. I thank God for the opportunity to debut my second television talk show, and I'm getting ready to launch a national women's magazine called *L: The Leslie Magazine*.

Never give up! You must stand the test of time. Hold onto the promise Christ made to you and persevere with faith. Just know that whatever you're going through God's dream for your life is so much greater! In everything you do and with everyone you meet from day to day make certain to have an "I Got It Moment."[10]

When we recognize that Christ is our Creator, Redeemer, and the One who holds our life together, we begin to "get it," as Leslie described. We grow to understand that God doesn't waste our pain, but uses each challenge in our lives to help us grow wiser and stronger. He does not leave us even when we can't feel Him or see Him. He holds us in His hand. Psalm 37 reminds us, "The LORD directs the steps of the godly. He delights in every detail of their lives. Though they stumble, they will never fall, for the LORD holds them by the hand."[11]

Not Just a Nice Guy

Let's not be fooled into thinking what some people want us to think, that Jesus was just a nice guy. Okay, yes—He was a nice guy, but He was and is so much more! I don't call myself a Christian just because I follow some "nice guy." I call myself a Christian because I have placed my faith in God's Son, who died for me on the cross. My hope is not built on a nice guy. My hope is built on the powerful Son of God who is all man and all God and who willingly sacrificed His life for us so we who believe may spend eternity with Him. The Bible says, "Salvation is found in no one else, for there is no other name under heaven given to men by which we must be saved."[12] Let's examine a few more of the attributes Paul proclaimed in our passage.

He is the head of the church. If you have ever been hurt by the church or disillusioned by church people, then this may not sound like a great title to you. When you think of the church, don't just think of a religion or a building or a denomination. The church is the body of believers; all those who have placed their faith in Christ. With Christ as our head, we are under His authority. The word *head* actually means source or origin as well as leader or ruler. The church began with Christ, and we still look to Christ as our authority and leader.

If we consider the illustration of the body and the head, then just as the head (the brain) controls every part of the body, so Christ controls every part of the body of believers. Where the head decides to go, the body follows. The hands and feet are useful parts of the body that carry out tasks, but each part falls under the direction of the head. Cults are usually centered around a *person* as their leader instead of Christ. As the body of Christ, we must look to Christ for our direction, leadership, and authority. Certainly God has placed people in positions of leadership within the body, and they must answer to Christ as well. The message to each of as believers is to follow Christ's leadership in our life. Look to Him, listen to Him, and obey Him. As a body of believers, work together in love under His authority.

He is the firstborn of all who will rise from the dead. Remember that the term *firstborn* means the principal figure or privileged one. Christ was the first to be resurrected and not die again. The supernatural beauty of the resurrection is that it establishes His authority over death, and it serves as a reminder that we look forward to a resurrected body one day. Death is not the end. He rose from the dead, declaring victory over the grave. We can rejoice in the glorious fact that death is not final. We can live with resurrection confidence, knowing we do not need to fear death.

The power of the resurrection gives us confidence not only for our future, but also for our lives right here and right now. We serve a risen savior, and the same Spirit who raised Christ from the dead lives within us. The power of the resurrection was not simply something that happened at the tomb; it affects our lives today as we live in His strength. In the book of Romans we read what the power of the resurrection means to us as believers,

If Christ is in you, your body is dead because of sin, yet your spirit is alive because of righteousness. And if the Spirit of him who raised Jesus from the dead is living in you, he who raised Christ from the dead will also give life to your mortal bodies through his Spirit, who lives in you. [13]

Because of the resurrection, we are able to experience abundant life here, as well as eternal life in heaven. The Spirit who raised Christ from the dead lives within us! What confidence we have knowing this! We are not alone. We are not powerless against sin. We have a Helper and Comforter who strengthens us and leads us.

In everything He has the supremacy. Absolute supremacy! Sounds like an Arnold Schwarzenegger movie, doesn't it? Jesus is supreme over all creation on earth and over the spirit world. He is supreme or first over—not some things, not almost all things—He is first over everything! Imagine an athlete who placed first in every track event. Wouldn't you want to be on his team? As believers in Christ, we are on His team! Other religions claim they follow a prophet or worship many gods. Some claim to follow certain systems or forms of enlightenment. Paul made it unequivocally clear—Jesus is above all.

There is great comfort in placing your faith in Christ, the one and only supreme God. Worry and fear no longer need to grip us when we recognize the greatness of the Christ who loves us. G. Campbell Morgan said, "The man who measures things by the circumstances of the hour is filled with fear; the man who sees Jehovah enthroned and governing has no panic."[14] When it seems like life is spinning out of control, we know the One who is over all things and we can take our cares directly to Him.

All of God's fullness dwells in Him and through Him. The totality of divine qualities has its permanent residency in Christ. The word for "fullness" is *pleroma*, which was often used by the Gnostics to refer to the sum or total of all divine power. The Gnostics said Jesus did not have this *pleroma*, or fullness of God, in Him. Paul put a stop to this nonsense in no uncertain terms. The Christians needed to understand that God's fullness lived in Christ and through Him. Later in Colossians Paul uses the word *pleroma* again when he declares, "In Christ all the fullness of the deity lives in bodily form."

Jesus was God incarnate, God in the flesh. This is why Jesus Himself said, "Anyone who has seen me has seen the Father." And again He said, "I am in the Father and the Father is in me."[15] Jesus was God in human form. If you ever encounter someone who questions His deity, I would take them to these passages. Not only did all the fullness of God live in and through Jesus, but Paul also said in Colossians that we have been given fullness in Christ.[16] Wow—that's both humbling and overwhelming at the same time. We as Christ's followers should show the world what Jesus looks like, just as He showed us what God looks like. Do others see the fullness of God in our lives? Do they feel the warmth of His love through our love and kindness?

> *Father, shine brightly through me, and please*
> *don't let my sinful and selfish desires get in the way*
> *of demonstrating Your love to the world.*

God reconciled all things to Himself through Christ by making peace through His blood shed on the cross. Herein is the gospel. God restored us to a right relationship with Him. How? By Christ's shed blood on the cross—not by our own works of righteousness, but by His work on the cross. He exchanged our sin for His righteousness. We are at peace with God through faith in what Christ did for us. Oh, the deep,

deep love of God, to make a way for us to be reconciled to Him! Oh, the precious blood of Christ shed on the cross for our behalf! God paid a great cost on our behalf. We are loved.

Why a blood sacrifice? Why did Jesus have to shed His own blood on the cross? In the Old Testament we read that God provided a way to atone for sins through the sacrifices of animals. It sounds awful, yet the awfulness of sin had to be paid for so God's people would be made right with Him. God in His loving-kindness put an end to the animal sacrifices once and for all by sending the perfect sacrifice, Jesus. Jesus' death on the cross was the final sacrifice. Jesus proclaimed from the cross, "It is finished." The debt of sin had been paid through His willing sacrifice. Greater love has no man than this, that he lay his life down for a friend. Jesus laid down His life for you and for me. There is no greater love.

Jesus was God's gift to the world. "God so loved the world that he gave his one and only son, that whoever believes in him shall not perish but have eternal life. For God did not send his Son into the world to condemn the world, but to save the world through him. Whoever believes in him is not condemned, but whoever does not believe stands condemned already because he has not believed in the name of God's one and only Son."[17] How wonderful to know the love of God and receive the gift He has given this world!

You don't earn a gift, you receive it. The Bible says, "It is by grace you have been saved, through faith—and this not from yourselves, it is the gift of God—not by works, so that no one can boast."[18] We are saved by God's grace. As we place our faith in Christ, we are no longer condemned, we are forgiven. We can have an eternal confidence, knowing that our sins are forgiven and we will live with Him one day in glory. Could there be any greater love? Walk confidently in His love, my friend.

Confident Steps

ADDITIONAL READING: John 1—God became flesh

BATTLE FOR THE TRUTH:

Confidence Defeater—*I'm a mistake. There is no purpose for my life.*

Confidence Builder—As believers in Christ we can be confident that the Almighty God created us for a purpose and has our lives in His hands.

CHOICES:

- Recognize Jesus as the exact image of God.
- Trust Him as your Creator.
- Thank God every day for creating you and for the plan He has for you.
- Look to Him as the One who holds your life together.
- Praise Him for His supremacy over all creation.
- Believe Him for your salvation.
- Seek His direction, comfort, and help.
- Respect all of creation.
- Believe in the Lord Jesus, who gave His life as payment for your sin.
- Walk in eternal confidence, knowing you are loved and not condemned.

DELIBERATE PLAN: Meditate on the truths about Christ.

In this chapter we learned life-changing truths concerning who Christ is and what He means to us personally. I want to encourage you to deliberately meditate on each one of these aspects of Christ. Take one of the attributes listed below and let it be your focus for an entire week. Write it on an index card and put it on your bathroom mirror or kitchen sink. Journal about what you learn as you dwell on each truth. Try to look for opportunities to talk about Christ's attributes throughout the week with family and friends. Thank God for each attribute as you meditate on it. Here is the list:

- He is the visible image of the invisible God.
- He is the firstborn (supreme) over all creation.
- By Him all things were created.
- He existed before everything else began.
- He holds all creation together.
- He is the head of the church.
- He is the firstborn of all who will rise from the dead.
- In everything He has the supremacy—He is supreme over all, the first in everything.
- All God's fullness dwells in Him and through Him.
- God reconciled all things through Christ, by making peace through His blood shed on the cross.

CHAPTER FOUR

mbracing the Lover of Your Soul

"This is how God showed his love among us:
He sent his one and only Son into the world
that we might live through him."

1 JOHN 4:9

"The most important thing in our Christian lives
is not how we look in our own sight or in the sight
of others, but how we look in God's sight."

WARREN W. WIERSBE

A number of years ago two young people went on a mission jour-ney to a small village in South Korea, a place where the gospel had never been preached. News spread quickly throughout the region of their arrival, and it seemed as though the entire population came out to hear their message. As the two faithfully shared the story of God's love and the truth about Jesus, the people listened intently and asked many penetrating questions. The meeting went on late into the night. Finally the exhausted missionaries closed down the meeting so they could get some rest. They were given a small room adjoining the meeting hall and tried their best to go to sleep, but the villagers kept murmuring and talking in the other room.

At about two o'clock in the morning, unable to sleep, the tired and frustrated missionaries decided to go back into the room and find out why the people were still there talking with each other. The head man of the village answered them, "How can we sleep? You have told us that the Supreme Power is not an evil spirit trying to injure us, but a loving God who gave His only begotten Son for our salvation, and that if we turn away from our sins and trust Him, we may have the deliverance from fear, guidance in our perplexities, comfort in our sorrows. How can we sleep after a message like this?"

The two missionaries got over being tired real quick! Energized by the villagers' interest, they sat down with their new Korean friends and talked about the treasure of knowing Jesus throughout the rest of the night.[1] Oh, the joy of the gospel message! Don't you wish we had the same excitement about the gospel as these people had? I dare say that most of us would hardly stay up all night to read a gripping novel or watch a favorite movie or DVD. But stay up all night just to talk about Jesus? These people were excited! And well they should have been. When you consider God's great love for us and how we are forgiven and can live fruitful and abundant lives in Christ, it is exciting. But let's be honest, I think most people live as though the honeymoon phase of being a Christian has faded into a dull routine of going to church and maybe doing a Bible study or two. The thrill is gone, the novelty has worn off, and the initial joy has definitely diminished.

It doesn't have to be this way. The gospel is thrilling! It is over-the-top, stay-up-all-night exciting to think of the love the Father has for us! It is my hope that as you read this chapter you will experience a fresh wind and a new fire for Christ. Hold on—I'm going to take it one step further and say, I believe this chapter will change the way you see yourself and talk to yourself! It will open your eyes to the Lover of your soul, so you see yourself as God sees you. This may be one of the most freeing, fulfilling, and life-changing chapters you have ever read. God's message found in Colossians is going to give you a before-and-after picture to help you truly appreciate the transformation Christ has done in your life.

What You Were

Most of us went through a few "ugly years." You know, the time in your growing-up years when you looked just plain embarrassing. For most of us it was during those awkward middle-school years. Personally, I find it's still painful to look back at my pictures from those years. My nose was way too big for the rest of my face, my braces made my mouth look like lip surgery gone bad. Let's not talk about my eyes. It was my first attempt at makeup, and I think I may have gone a little overboard with the blue mascara and eyeliner. And why did my mom let me wear my hair like that? Probably because I argued with her until I wore her down. Thank goodness we didn't stay in that stage forever.

In a similar way, before we knew Christ we were in an ugly stage. If you have forgotten about the ugliness of those years, Paul reminds us with a little snapshot. Here's the picture he gives of our spiritually ugly years before we knew Christ:

COLOSSIANS 1:21

Once you were alienated from God and were enemies in your minds because of your evil behavior.

Now you may be thinking, *Not me! I wasn't that bad of a person before I knew Christ.* You may not have been bad on the outside, but Paul is describing a spiritual condition on the inside. I know, because I was one of those "good little girls" who did everything right in my actions, but I was ugly on the inside and didn't know Christ. Paul used the word "alienated," which means "estranged." We were separated from God. Our sin separates us from God. In other words, sin alienates us from the Father. In Paul's letter to the Romans we read, "The sinful mind is hostile to God. It does not submit to God's law, nor can it do so. Those controlled by the sinful nature cannot please God."[2]

I don't want to be a Debbie Downer talking about how bad off we were. But if we are going to understand how great God's love is toward us, we must first get the picture of how very far we were from God. Yes, we were in enemy territory. We were enemies in our minds. Our minds are a battlefield, aren't they? In our minds we can harbor hatred and bitterness toward both God and man. In our minds we can build up self-hatred. Our minds are important to God. He wants us to love Him with all of our mind. Before we came to know Christ, our minds didn't understand the love God had for us. In fact, one of the biggest lies we can believe is that God couldn't possibly love us. But when we come to understand the love of God in all its truth, our minds begin to change.

What You Are

Even though we were separated from God and enemies in our minds, God reached down and loved us. Not only does He love us with an unfailing love, but He has made us holy in His sight. Read on:

COLOSSIANS 1:22

But now he has reconciled you by Christ's physical body through death to present you holy in his sight, without blemish and free from accusation.

In my ugly years, those pitiful middle-school years, there was one thing I wanted. Well, actually two things. I wanted a boyfriend, but even more than that I wanted to be without blemish. Yes, I failed to mention earlier that my ugliness was enhanced by acne. I tried everything, but those ugly zits just wouldn't go away. Finally my mother had mercy on me and took me to a dermatologist, who gave me some lotion for my skin. And he also gave me a low dose of antibiotics to take care of the infection underneath the skin. Soon I was smiling (with those lovely metal braces, no less) because my face was clear, without blemish. I wish I could say things went as well in the boyfriend category, but one wish out of two wasn't bad.

Through Christ's death on the cross we are without blemish (not the facial kind but the spiritual kind) and free from accusation. Our life was completely covered in sin, but through Christ we have been cleaned up. He cleaned us up on the inside and got rid of the infection of sin once and for all in our lives. We are holy in His sight. That's amazing. *You mean to tell me when God looks at me He sees a clean and forgiven person?* Yes, as a believer in Christ we have been reconciled, made right with God. We are no longer alienated or separated from Him. The Bible tells us there is no condemnation for those who are in Christ Jesus.[3]

But I still sin. How can I be holy and free from accusation if I still sin? Because the punishment for our sin, the condemnation, was placed on Christ. He bore the penalty of our sin on the cross. We still sin, and we will still experience some of the natural consequences of our sin, but our spiritual status is forgiven. Just as in a court of law—when a judge declares a person not guilty, they are acquitted of all accusations and charges. In a legal sense it is as if the crime was never committed. The best illustration I ever heard was taught by a pastor I heard when I was growing up.

He told the story of a little boy who was watching a parade with his dad. They were inside a store, watching through the store's giant plate-glass window. At one point the father exclaimed, "Oh, look at those bright red uniforms on the band members." But the little boy said, "I don't see red uniforms, I see white uniforms." The dad replied, "No, son, they are red. Can't you see that they are bright red?" It was at that moment the father looked down and noticed that his son was observing the parade through a piece of red cellophane that was part of the store's window advertisement. Now when you look at white and red objects through red cellophane, they all seem the same, giving the impression that they are all white. Just as the boy saw only white uniforms through the red cellophane, God looks at us through Christ's blood and sees us as clean and forgiven.

The Accuser

Since we have already opened up the ugly chapter of my middle-school years, I thought I would share with you a painful memory. You see, being a fair-skinned, blonde-haired girl, I had a blushing problem. Really, my face turned bright red whenever I had to get up in front of the class to give a speech. It was horrible, not because my face looked so bad, but because some of the kids would laugh hysterically at me whenever I gave a speech. There was a group of boys who seemed to look forward to each time I had to stand in front of the class just to see how very red my face would become. I guess my blushing made a good form of entertainment in an otherwise boring class.

Even in the hallways outside of class the boys would point to me and yell, "There goes the red-faced girl." Let's just say those weren't my fondest middle-school memories. Their accusations and name-calling helped deplete my confidence level to zero. It is a wonder that I get up and speak in front of groups today. How did I move beyond the ridicule? I had to change my focus and my thinking. I was only focused on what everyone thought about me and the fact that my face would turn bright red again and again. But when I started focusing on my speech and the information I was talking about and got my mind off those boys, I became less and less nervous. When I wasn't thinking about me, my fears subsided. Eventually the accusers stopped, and my confidence grew.

The Bible reminds us that Satan, our enemy, is an accuser. He would love for us to believe we are worthless and to doubt God's love and forgiveness toward us. He doesn't want us to recognize that we have been reconciled to God through Christ. And so we hear his voice whispering in our ear, "How can you be holy in God's sight after what you did? People who are reconciled to God don't lie or cheat or get mad when they're cut off in traffic. God's people surely don't argue with their spouse or gossip about neighbors or get frustrated because they don't get the raise they wanted. Oh no, you couldn't possibly be holy in His sight." And as we listen to that voice, our level of confidence as God's beloved child goes to zero.

We must not listen to the accuser's voice—we must listen instead to God's voice. What does His Word tell us? Say it with me: "He has reconciled you by Christ's physical body through death to present you holy in his sight, without blemish and free from accusation." The accuser doesn't want us to focus on what Christ has done for us and where we stand in Him. There is great joy in knowing we are reconciled to God. Do not let the accuser rob you of that joy. The Bible reminds us,

> *God showed his great love for us by sending Christ to die for us while*
> *we were still sinners. And since we have been made right in God's sight*

> by the blood of Christ, he will certainly save us from God's condem-
> nation. For since our friendship with God was restored by the death
> of his Son while we were still his enemies, we will certainly be saved
> through the life of his Son. So now we can rejoice in our wonderful
> new relationship with God because our Lord Jesus Christ has made
> us friends of God. [4]

No longer enemies, but friends! Oh, the joy of knowing that God
has brought us into a relationship with Him. He has exchanged our
filthy rags of sin for clean clothes of righteousness. Through Christ's
death on the cross, God has dismissed our penalty of sin. He has
acquitted us and declared us not guilty. I remember, as a girl, seeing
pictures of American prisoners of war in Vietnam as they were set free
from years of imprisonment—beaten, hungry, and clothed in rags. Yet
when they were rescued they were given food, medical aid, and clean
clothes. They were released, set free, and no longer obligated to carry
out their sentence. Relief and joy were evident on each face. The enemy
no longer had power over them.

Let's not confuse the accuser's voice with God's gentle spirit of conviction. God's Spirit lovingly leads us back to Him because His way is
always the best way for us to live. There is great joy in living in obedience to God. But the accuser's voice is harsh and demeaning, making
us doubt that we are God's. How do you discern between healthy conviction and accusing guilt? We can identify a voice by certain qualities.
Always keep in mind the following characteristics:

God's Spirit	*Satan's Accusations*
Points you back to God's love	Make you feel unloved by God
Points you toward righteousness	Make you feel guilty that you failed
Reminds you of God's power	Make you feel unworthy
Reminds you of God's presence	Make you feel abandoned by God

Reminds you of redemption	Make you feel like you are hopeless
Points you to the truth in the Bible	Distract you with man's ideas

Our thought life plays a significant role in what we believe about ourselves and about others. We must be continually aware and discerning of the voice we listen to. The more we know God's Word, the more we recognize His voice. Don't let the accuser fill your mind with lies and rob you of the joy of being free and forgiven in Christ.

I also want to mention that we must guard against being an accuser toward others. Examine your own words and make sure you are not hurling accusations, blame, or ridicule at another person. We want to reflect Christ in our relationships. Focus on Christ, not on other people's sins and problems. It is the Holy Spirit's job to gently convict and help turn people from sin. Let Him do His work. There may be times when God leads us to confront a fellow sister or brother in Christ, but we must do that carefully and prayerfully, using the principles from Matthew 18:15-19 as our guide. Our job is to love others as our heavenly Father loves us, with a grace-filled, patient, forgiving love.

Firm and Established

One of my favorite prayers in the Bible talks about being strengthened in God's love and grasping the reality of how very much we are loved by God. Paul wrote it in his letter to the Ephesians, but I think we all need this prayer. I actually pray it quite often for family and friends and for myself. Here it is:

> *I pray that out of his glorious riches he may strengthen you with power through his Spirit in your inner being, so that Christ may dwell in your hearts through faith. And I pray that you, being rooted and established in love, may have power, together with all the saints, to grasp how wide and long and high and deep is the love of Christ, and to know this love that surpasses knowledge—that you may be filled to the measure of all the fullness of God.*

Now to him who is able to do immeasurably more than all we ask or imagine, according to his power that is at work within us, to him be glory in the church and in Christ Jesus throughout all generations, for ever and ever! Amen. [5]

I want to grasp how long and wide and high and deep God's love is, don't you? It is impossible to conceive of the vast storehouse of His abundant love. Paul wanted Christians to know and grasp the wonderful truth of God's powerful love because he knew it would change their thinking and their actions. He talked about being "rooted and established in love," and he uses that same term in speaking about the faith of the Colossians. It was an architectural image, like a house firmly set on a foundation.

COLOSSIANS 1:23

...if you continue in your faith, established and firm, not moved from the hope held out in the gospel. This is the gospel that you heard and that has been proclaimed to every creature under heaven, and of which I, Paul, have become a servant.

The Colossians could understand the importance of a good foundation because they were located in a region known for its earthquakes. The words "not moved" could be translated "not earthquake-stricken." In 2010 we watched in horror and sadness as we saw the crumbled buildings in Haiti after the tragic earthquake there. Other earthquakes of similar magnitude have occurred around the world, yet the devastation and loss of life was not as great. Why was the loss in Haiti so pronounced? One of the reasons is that the buildings were not built to withstand an earthquake.

Paul didn't want the Colossians' faith to crumble and fall apart upon the eruption of deceptive philosophies. The only way for them to build a sound structure was to build their faith on the truth of the gospel and the understanding of God's love and grace. We too must build our confidence on the firm foundation of God's truth and love. We must know who He is and what He has done for us on the cross. We must stand firm on this hope based on God's truth so we will not be swayed by man's ideas, which come and go with the culture. I love the old hymn by Edward Mote:

> My hope is built on nothing less
> than Jesus' blood and righteousness.
> I dare not trust the sweetest frame,
> but wholly lean on Jesus' name.
> On Christ, the solid Rock, I stand,
> all other ground is sinking sand.[6]

Where is your hope built? Is it established and firm on the sure foundation of Christ and what He did for you on the cross? Don't let the accuser shake you up and distract you from the truth of God's love. Don't let man's ideas and philosophies sway you and lead you down a different path or belief system. Stand firm in confidence in Christ! The gospel is unshakable.

Also, the gospel is not exclusive. The Gnostics prided themselves on having a secret spiritual knowledge, reserved only for the spiritually elite. Paul made it clear that the gospel was proclaimed to everyone. It didn't matter if you were Jew or gentile, circumcised or uncircumcised, barbarian, slave, or free, the gospel message was offered to everyone regardless of race or status. Paul said he had become a servant of the gospel. Paul's desire, like Christ's was to serve, not to be served. As we consider today's religious leaders, those who are proclaiming the gospel, we can only hope they see themselves in a similar role, as servants of the gospel.

Jesus said if we want to be great in God's kingdom we must learn to be the servant of all. Greatness does not come from having people serve us, it comes in lovingly serving others. Confidence is built not by looking out for my own interests, but by getting my eyes off myself and seeking to help others. Joy, confidence, and love all grow from a faith firmly rooted in the gospel and from understanding God's unshakable love for us. As we understand His love for us, we in turn can't help but pour that love out in grace-filled love and service for others. How blessed is the woman who lives confidently in Christ's love and shares that love with the world!

You are loved! You are free from accusation. You are holy in His sight! You are without blemish! Go ahead smile about that. Take a moment to thank God for His great love toward you. Ponder how long and wide and high and deep is His love for you—yes, you. Go ahead and smile again as you think about how dearly loved you are by God. Carry that smile throughout the day with you today and share it with someone who needs it.

Confident Steps

ADDITIONAL READING: Romans 8—Our foundation in Him

BATTLE FOR THE TRUTH:

Confidence Defeater—*I've done so many wrong things. God couldn't possibly love and forgive me.*

Confidence Builder—Our confidence is strengthened as we recognize in Christ we are holy in God's sight, free from accusation, and without blemish.

CHOICES:

- See yourself as God sees you, without blemish, free from accusation.
- Give thanks continually for what the Lord has done for you.
- Replace the enemy's accusations with God's truth.
- Listen to God's gentle and loving voice of conviction.
- Do not be an accuser of others.
- Live in the joy of knowing you are reconciled to God.
- Focus on others' needs.

DELIBERATE PLAN: Memorize Colossians 1:22.

He has reconciled you by Christ's physical body
through death to present you holy in his sight,
without blemish and free from accusation.

The best way to take a stand against the accusations of
the enemy is to focus on God's truth. One of the greatest
truths we can know is the truth of who we are in Christ. I
want to encourage you to write out Colossians 1:22 several
times on different index cards and place them throughout your house, in your purse, and on the dash of your car.
Phrase by phrase, practice saying the verse aloud every day.
Ask the Lord to help you hold it in your memory. Share
it with a family member in conversation. Personally, I like
to work on Scripture memory while I am working out, as
the rhythm and flow of oxygen seem to help my thinking.
Once you have it memorized, repeat it every morning as a
reminder of where you stand in Christ.

PART THREE

Step Forward

*"We are God's workmanship,
created in Christ Jesus to do good works,
which God prepared in advance for us to do."*

EPHESIANS 2:10

*"One can never consent to creep when
one feels an impulse to soar."*

HELEN KELLER

$\mathcal{H}$idden Treasures and Hope-Filled Dreams

"If anyone is in Christ, he is a new creation;
the old has gone, the new has come!
All this is from God, who reconciled
us to himself through Christ."

2 Corinthians 5:17-18

"The ground of our hope is Christ in the world,
but the evidence of our hope is Christ in the heart."

Matthew Henry

Hope is easy to promise but hard to deliver. People promise it in a myriad of ways. Politicians promise hope for the future. Doctors talk of hope for a cure. Financial analysts point toward hope for an economic upturn. Friends and family speak of hope as a form of well-wishes or encouragement. Yet when your life is falling apart or things are not going as you planned, the possibility of hope becomes vitally important in your life, and you don't take it lightly. Hope is much more than a warm fuzzy feeling and a happy expectation. True hope nourishes your soul, changes your perspective, and gives you the strength to persevere despite the circumstances.

Born in 1716 to a Baptist minister in Hampshire, England, Anne Steele suffered most of her life from poor health. Yet from her sickroom she composed volumes of writing under the pen name "Theodosia," which means "God's gift." Only one who has known suffering could write with such joy in her heart based on God's goodness. Her hope was not in her circumstances but in her God. You can sense her contentedness in these verses:

> Give me a calm, a thankful heart,
>   From ev'ry murmur free;
> The blessings of Thy grace impart,
>   And let me live to Thee.
>
> Let the sweet hope that Thou art mine,
>   My life and death attend,
> Thy presence through my journey shine,
>   And crown my journey's end.[1]

Ultimately, what does hope come down to? Certainly we can hope our circumstances and situations turn out well for us, but there are no guarantees. Even if our problems and pain and hurt aren't resolved, our hope is not lost, for hope is found in the God who loves us and is able to redeem any situation for good purposes. Hope in God lifts us from despair and gives us a deep sense of joy in knowing He can bring something good even from something awful.

Author Henri J.M. Nouwen talks about hope this way:

> When we live with hope we do not get tangled up with concerns for how our wishes will be fulfilled. So, too, our prayers are not directed toward the gift, but toward the one who gives it. Our prayers might still contain just as many desires, but ultimately it is not a question of having a wish come true but of expressing an unlimited faith in the giver of all good things.[2]

Paul's faith and hope was in the giver of all good things. He was confident that his life was in God's hands, and his hope was in Him. Paul had a deep sense of joy even as he suffered for the sake of Christ because his hope was not in his circumstances, but in the God who loved him. He learned to rejoice in the not-so-perfect situations in life. Chained to a prison guard he wrote,

COLOSSIANS 1:24

I rejoice in what was suffered for you, and I fill up in my flesh what is still lacking in regard to Christ's afflictions, for the sake of his body, which is the church.

He recognized that he could whine and complain about his suffering—or he could rejoice in the midst of it. God never wastes our pain. Paul's hope was in the Lord, and he knew God could do greater works beyond his sufferings. Paul was aware that his chains and imprisonment encouraged other Christians to speak the word of God more courageously and boldly. He also knew that his chains gave him the opportunity to slow down long enough to write some profound letters (which we are reading today) and minister one-on-one to his visitors, not to mention the palace guards who kept watch over him.

Paul realized he was experiencing the privilege of sharing in the sufferings of Christ. When Paul used the words "still lacking in regard to Christ's afflictions" he was not referring to the work of salvation Christ did on the cross. That work was complete from the moment Jesus said, "It is finished." Christ's sacrificial suffering is complete, but His body, the church, continues to experience suffering while here on earth. Paul found his comfort in Christ just as we can too. He wrote, "Just as the sufferings of Christ flow over into our lives, so also through Christ our comfort overflows."[3]

You may be in the midst of a difficult situation right now in your life. Perhaps you are suffering from the emotional pain of a broken relationship or the physical pain of a disability or disease. Take heart from the words of a fellow suffering servant, Paul, and recognize that even if you can't see any hope, God is with you. He has not left you, and He knows how it feels to suffer. He can bring hope from even the most difficult of circumstances—and most importantly, He can strengthen you and guide you along the way. Remember, our greatest hope still awaits us in glory. In Romans we read,

> We rejoice in the hope of the glory of God. Not only so, but we also rejoice in our sufferings, because we know that suffering produces perseverance; perseverance, character; and character, hope. And hope does not disappoint us, because God has poured out his love into our hearts by the Holy Spirit, whom he has given us. [4]

The Big Secret

A funny thing happened to me recently, and I can only assume that God must have orchestrated it so I could write about it in this book. I was in the middle of trying to study the next passage in Colossians, but I just couldn't seem to concentrate. It may have been because we had a bazillion workers at our house fixing the ceiling that had caved in during a rainstorm due to a leak in our roof. Oh yes, fun times! Never a dull moment at the Ladd house! After getting interrupted every few minutes, I decided to pack up my books and go to a local restaurant to finish my work. God uses our frustrations for greater purpose, as you will soon see.

I camped out at a table right beside a big planter and resumed my intensive studying. I started reading commentaries about the Gnostics of Paul's day and how they believed all these ridiculous ideas like secret knowledge and elite spiritual levels. It was hard for me to believe that anyone would buy into their system of philosophical beliefs. I wondered to myself, *Are there people who believe this kind of stuff today?* Well, God decided to answer that question for me right then and there. Remember the planter I sat down next to at the restaurant? There was a table on the other side of the planter, and two men sat down to eat and have a chat. I couldn't see them, but I sure could hear them!

One man began telling the other about a secret society of which he is a member. I'm not sure why he was talking so loudly if it was a *secret* society, but he was talking loudly enough for me to hear every single word. He said that there are hundreds of these secret societies and they have been around for ages and generations. They have different levels of knowledge, and those who have reached the high levels of maturity pass down the wisdom to those on lower levels. He then went on to inform his friend of one of the bits of mysterious wisdom. According to this guy we have different bubbles hovering around us, a negative one and a positive one. The more you feed the positive one, the more you get what you want. The energy in the universe aligns together to give it to you. But if you think negative thoughts then you weaken the energy.

My jaw dropped open! I couldn't believe it. Here I was studying Colossians, in which Paul is specifically refuting Gnostic beliefs about hidden societies and secret knowledge, and I'm sitting right next to a modern-day Gnostic type of guy. Some of the terms were very similar to those Paul used in Colossians. I wish I could tell you I went around to the other side of the planter and shared the truth of Christ with them and they both fell on their knees and believed—but I sort of missed my opportunity. While I was busy writing down as much as I could from the discourse, they finished talking and left. But just so you know, the one who was listening didn't buy into the secret society stuff. He basically told his Gnostic friend, "Well, that's nice if it works for you." I can imagine he was ready to get out of there pretty quick.

So now let's take a look at Paul's passage. Read it carefully, and we'll look at a few terms that are still popping up in today's philosophical circles.

Colossians 1:25-29

I have become its [the church's] servant by the commission God gave me to present to you the word of God in its fullness—the mystery that has been kept hidden for ages and generations, but is now disclosed to the saints. To them God has chosen to make known among the Gentiles the glorious riches of this mystery, which is Christ in you, the hope of glory.

We proclaim him, admonishing and teaching everyone with all wisdom, so that we may present everyone perfect in Christ. To this end I labor, struggling with all his energy, which so powerfully works in me.

The words "mystery," "hidden," and "perfect" were all juicy terms to the Gnostics, so Paul used their language to help the Colossians understand the mystery of Christ.

Mystery to us may seem like a word that describes a suspense novel, but in Paul's day the false teachers used it to describe the inner secrets of their religions. It referred to a holy or sacred secret that was kept *hidden*, but was revealed only to a special group. In this passage Paul is describing God's sacred secret, which was the saving grace of Christ to all who believe. Christ was prophesied about in the Old Testament, and now He was revealed. Paul made a special emphasis that this ministry was not for the Jews only, but also for the Gentiles. The Gnostic mysteries were confined to a small, elite group, but Christ was proclaimed to all.

Perfect was a term the Gnostics used to describe the disciple who had matured and was fully instructed in the mysteries and secrets of the religion. They were no longer a novice but rather were enlightened. Paul used the same word to mean *complete in Christ*. We are holy—without blemish, forgiven. This is what he was working toward, presenting everyone perfect in Christ. Paul said he did all this with God's energy, which so powerfully worked within him. Keep in mind that this same power is at work within us as well. Don't miss the important truth that we are complete in Christ, and He has given us everything we need for living a godly life. It wasn't just Paul the apostle who served in God's strength; it isn't just mega-missionaries or super-preachers who serve in God's strength. God has equipped each of us with the ability and the power to carry out the work He has given us.

To me the most glorious and wonderful sentence in all of Colossians is, "To them [the saints] God has chosen to make known among the Gentiles the glorious riches of this mystery, which is Christ in you, the hope of glory." Isn't it wonderful that God chose to make Christ known to the Gentiles? Yes, if God had kept Christ only for the Jewish nation, then where would we be?

> *Oh, praise You, Father, for inviting us*
> *to be a part of Your family!*

Notice Paul uses the term "glorious riches." *Glorious* in Hellenistic Greek terms meant "bright light" and referred to divine disclosure or revelation of God. *Riches,* of course, implies wealth. God has allowed us to be spiritually wealthy by allowing us to know Christ. Christ in us! Are we not rich? Are we not completely wealthy to have the spirit of Christ within us? Christ has freely been given to us by our loving heavenly Father.

We can have hope of glory because Christ dwells in us. And certainly we look forward to that day when we will be with Him in glory. We are able to press on, knowing that this is not our home. We know that glory awaits us. We can be confident in that hope. In Ephesians we are reminded that we are sealed until the day of redemption because God's Spirit lives inside us. Read it here in *The Message* paraphrase:

> *It's in Christ that we find out who we are and what we are living for. Long before we first heard of Christ and got our hopes up, he had his eye on us, had designs on us for glorious living, part of the overall purpose he is working out in everything and everyone.*
>
> *It's in Christ that you, once you heard the truth and believed it (this Message of your salvation), found yourselves home free—signed, sealed, and delivered by the Holy Spirit. This signet from God is the first installment on what's coming, a reminder that we'll get everything God has planned for us, a praising and glorious life.* [5]

Play Money vs. True Treasure

When my daughters were little we used to play "Go to the Movies." We set up our family room to look like a movie theater, complete with concession stand and ticket taker. I rented a movie, popped popcorn, and pulled out some old holiday candy, and we pretended we were actually at the theater. The girls used play money to buy their tickets, popcorn, drinks, and candy. It was a good way to teach them about money as well as have some special time together watching a movie. I don't remember the exact day they realized that the play money wouldn't get them anywhere in the real world, but eventually, they grew out of play money (and all too early, in my opinion).

You know, some play money can look so real, but it has absolutely no value. Paul was concerned that the Colossians were being fooled by fake treasures. He didn't want them to be deceived by play money in the form of fine-sounding arguments when true spiritual riches could be found in Christ. Secret treasures of wisdom and knowledge were enticing, yet they had no substance. Paul's desire was for them to have the full riches of complete understanding so that they might know Christ, in whom are hidden all the real treasures of wisdom and knowledge. Here's how Paul expressed his struggle:

COLOSSIANS 2:1-5

I want you to know how much I am struggling for you and for those at Laodicea, and for all who have not met me personally. My purpose is that they may be encouraged in heart and united in love, so that they may have the full riches of complete understanding, in order that they may know the mystery of God, namely, Christ, in whom are hidden all the treasures of wisdom and knowledge. I tell you this so that no one may deceive you by fine-sounding arguments. For though I am absent from you in body, I am present with you in spirit and delight to see how orderly you are and how firm your faith in Christ is.

If you have been given true treasure, why would you play with fake money? It doesn't make sense—unless you don't recognize the glorious riches of the treasure you have. Do you recognize the true treasure you have in Christ? All the sacred secrets of divine wisdom are found in Him. You don't need to look any further. He answers every question. How must a person inherit eternal life? Through faith in Him. How can a person experience deep and abiding joy? By knowing His love. How does a woman experience lasting confidence? By recognizing Christ created her, redeemed her, and has a good purpose for her. How can we find strength to make it through difficulties? We can do this through Christ, who strengthens us. How can we learn to love others? Christ showed us what love looks like, and He pours His love through us. How can we forgive? Through the power of Christ, because He forgave us all our sins.

Do you see how very rich you are? You are overwhelmingly wealthy with glorious riches. He is our treasure. In Christ we find our salvation, our purpose, our anchor, our direction, our comfort. I love what Paul said in his letter to the Ephesians, "In him we have redemption through his blood, the forgiveness of sins, in accordance with the riches of God's grace that he lavished on us with all wisdom and understanding." Did you read that? God lavished on us the riches of His grace with all wisdom and insight. God didn't hold back—He generously gave of His grace and wisdom.

When I think of the riches of God's wisdom I'm reminded of the doxology we read in Romans:

> *Oh, the depth of the riches of the wisdom and knowledge of God!*
> > *How unsearchable his judgments,*
> > *And his paths beyond tracing out!*
> *Who has known the mind of the Lord?*
> > *Or who has been his counselor?*
> *Who has ever given to God,*
> > *That God should repay him?*
> *For from him and through him and to him are all things.*
> > *To him be the glory forever! Amen.* [6]

Christ is our all in all. He is our rock, our strength, our hope, our comfort. He is wisdom and knowledge. Do you need direction in your life? Do you need guidance? Seek His face. He invites us to come to Him. Oh my sister, we have a treasure chest of His glorious riches. Why do we look other places, when all our answers are found in Him?

— *Confident Steps* —

ADDITIONAL READING: Ephesians 1—Spiritual riches in Christ

BATTLE FOR THE TRUTH:

Confidence defeater: *I have no source of direction or hope.*

Confidence Builder—We can enjoy the confidence of knowing we are spiritually wealthy and completely satisfied in Christ.

CHOICES:

- Find your hope in Christ and not in circumstances.
- Rejoice in the Lord always.
- Recognize the power of God working in you.
- Don't be deceived by fine-sounding arguments.
- Remember you are spiritually rich in Him.
- Discover the treasures of wisdom and knowledge in Christ.

DELIBERATE PLAN: Seeking the treasures of His wisdom.

In the book of James we read, "If any of you lacks wisdom, he should ask God, who gives generously to all without finding fault, and it will be given to him." Consider where you are struggling right now and in need of God's wisdom and direction. Take your concern to the Lord, who generously gives to all. Seek His wisdom and direction, and be alert for His answers through His Word, wise counsel, or His still small voice. Write out your thoughts below.

I need wisdom concerning: _____

_____.

Direction that God is giving me: _____

_____

_____.

CHAPTER SIX

*C*onfidently
Walking with Christ

*"It is for freedom that Christ has set us free.
Stand firm, then, and do not let yourselves
be burdened again by a yoke of slavery."*

GALATIANS 5:1

*"God is not waiting to show us strong in his behalf,
but himself strong in our behalf.
That makes a lot of difference.
He is not out to demonstrate what we can do
but what he can do."*

VANCE HAVNER

W hen the Robersons moved into a house not too far from ours, we were thrilled. It's always fun to have dear friends living close by, and especially if they give you their trees. Let me explain. You see, they didn't like the landscaping around their house and wanted to get rid of a few Savannah holly trees. Being the kind and thoughtful friends we are, we volunteered to take the trees off their hands and plant them in our own yard. Wow, what a deal—free trees! We found just the right spot for them. Our house backs up to a pleasant little creek, and so we planted them near the creek to enhance the beauty of the area. Five lovely Savannah hollies lining our creek! We were so proud of ourselves.

The water in our creek tends to rise when we have a rainstorm, and boy, did we have a gully washer one night right after we planted those hollies. On the morning after the storm, we woke up and looked out our window. *Hmm,* we wondered, *what were those large holes in the ground? Wait a minute—and where were our hollies?* Three of them were completely gone! Yes, swept away! We had another storm soon after that, and guess what? The other two were swept downstream too. Oh, well—easy come, easy go.

Now if the hollies had been given the time to take root they might have stayed around, but since they were newly planted there was nothing to hold them in the ground as the water rose and the current flowed. If you have ever watched floodwaters rise, then you know the strength and power of the current. It will sweep away anything and everything that is not deeply rooted or firmly founded in the ground. Large objects can be carried miles away downstream. The same is true with the flow of religious ideas and philosophies and the current of our society. If we are not deeply rooted in the truth of Christ, we can easily be carried away by concepts and ideas that sound good and seem valid.

Paul's words to the Colossians are just as important and timely for us today. There is a constant flow of ideas that "sound right," and "seem good." But we must know *the* truth, *God's* truth. Jesus said, "If you hold to my teaching, you are really my disciples. Then you will know the truth, and the truth will set you free."[1]As we hold to God's teaching and are rooted and built up in Him, then we will be free from the pull and drag of man-made rules and fine-sounding philosophies. Here is Paul's encouragement to the Colossians:

COLOSSIANS 2:6-8

So then, just as you received Christ Jesus as Lord, continue to live in him, rooted and built up in him, strengthened in the faith as you were taught, and overflowing with thankfulness. See to it that no one takes you captive through hollow and deceptive philosophy, which depends on human tradition and the basic principles of this world rather than on Christ.

Power Walk

Walking is the new running; at least it is for Curt and me. At one time we ran long-distance races, but now our knees won't let us, and so we walk. Some fitness experts say that walking is better for you as it doesn't jar your body, and you can go for longer periods of time. Curt and I agree that it works for us because it is easier to get up early in the morning, put on our shoes, and get right into walking. We actually look forward to it. Running? Not so much. Paul used a walking term as he encouraged the Colossians' growth in their relationship with Christ. He said since we have received Christ (trusted Him in faith) we should *live* in Him. The word "live" in the original Greek is *peripateo*, meaning "to tread all around, walk at large." Figuratively it meant to live in, or to follow as a companion.

When we trust Christ, we receive Him into our lives. His spirit comes to dwell within us. We are to walk together in step with Him. Let me give you an example. Let's say you decide you are going to start walking every morning, so you order a pair of walking shoes online. When you receive them you put them on. Then what do you do? Do you just stand there at the door and say, "I'm a walker. I've received walking shoes." That would be ridiculous! No, you go outside, and you begin walking in your shoes. Yet how many Christians say, "I'm a Christian; I have received Christ"—but when it comes to walking in Him and living in Him day by day, well…they kind of ignore Him?

In a practical sense, what does it mean to walk with Christ? If we continue reading this verse we can get a good idea of what walking with Him looks like. Paul said we ought to be rooted and built up in Him. I don't know about you, but I'm seeing two directions here. Roots go down deep in the ground and buildings go up in the sky. Let's talk about the roots first. They are the unseen part of the plant, yet they are where the plant or tree gets its strength and nourishment. Like my long-gone Savannah hollies, if our roots do not go down deep we can be carried away quite easily. So we develop strength and depth through the study of God's Word and through prayer. These are those unseen activities in the quiet places that are between you and God. I'm convinced that the reason many Christians are not more deeply rooted in Christ is because they avoid the work done in the solitude of the quiet place, where no one else sees us but God. It's where true depth in Christ and knowledge of Him grow.

The term "built up in Him" is an architectural term. We are to be built up in Christ. "Up" is a positive term, isn't it? Many times people think of Christianity in negative terms: "You can't do this; you can't do that." Paul told us to be *built* up, not *guilt* up! Being built up and strengthened in Him is obviously a positive term. Now we can be built up by the world in a number of different ways, from prestigious awards to flattering words, but Paul tells us to be built up *in Christ*. So we must first ask ourselves, "Is Christ my foundation?" Every building needs to begin on a sure foundation. We must consider if we are building our lives on Christ and the foundation of His Word.

Is there evidence of our edifice? If we are being built up in Him, strengthened by His Spirit, there will be evidence in our lives. Can others see Jesus in our actions and our words? Remember what the fruit of God's Spirit dwelling in us looks like: love, joy, peace, patience, kindness, goodness, faithfulness, gentleness, and self-control. These wonderful fruits are produced by Christ's Spirit in our lives as we live in Him. Jesus said, "I am the vine, you are the branches. He who abides in Me, and I in him, bears much fruit; for without me you can do nothing."[2] We can choose to be built up in Him, finding our confidence and strength in Him, or we can choose to live our lives trying to please others. One is a sure foundation; the other is shaky.

As our power walk continues and we examine what it means to walk in Christ, we read the words, "strengthened in your faith as you were taught." How is your faith being strengthened? Are you learning from good, sound, biblical teachers? In order for a child to be strengthened, she must be fed, and in order for our faith to be strengthened, we must be fed as well. What kind of food are you listening to in order to help your faith grow? I want to encourage you to continually learn and grow in your knowledge of God's Word through personal study as well as great Bible teaching. The more we know the Bible, the stronger our faith becomes.

Finally, our power walk ends with these words: "and overflowing with thankfulness." Just this morning, Curt and I went on a walk in the 101-degree heat in Dallas. I wasn't overflowing with thankfulness, but I was overflowing with sweat! Well, really, "glistening" is the term I prefer to use. Curt sweats; I glisten. Whatever we want to call it, it is a natural overflow from walking in the heat. Now, on a more positive and delightful note, as we are rooted in Christ thankfulness should overflow from every part of our life. When things are going well, we need to overflow with thankfulness, which I dare say we rarely do. Now here's the real kicker—when things are worrisome or difficult, we need to overflow with thankfulness. Yes, we are to give thanks in every situation.

Now perhaps you are wondering how in the world you can give thanks when your life is falling apart. Here are a few ways to begin:

> *Thank You, Father, that You are with me and have never left me.*
>
> *Thank You, Lord, that this situation is no surprise to You and You are in control.*
>
> *Thank You, Father, that You are my creator and comforter and You know what I need.*
>
> *Thank You that You are a redeeming God and You can bring hope to this situation.*
>
> *Thank You, Father, for You can use this difficulty for greater good in my life.*
>
> *Thank You, Father, as You can use this to touch other people's lives as well.*
>
> *Thank You, Lord, that You invite me to cast my cares on You because You care for me.*
>
> *Thank You, Lord, that You are all-wise and all-knowing.*
>
> *Thank You, Lord, that You are always teaching me through my challenges and mistakes.*

I could go on and on, but I think you get the point. The power walk Paul laid out for us is a walk of confidence, based on a life lived in Him. Notice the repetition of "in Him." We walk confidently when we are walking in Him, rooted in Him, built up in Him, strengthened in our faith in Him, and overflowing with thankfulness in Him! In Christ we live and move and have our being. Don't just put on your walking shoes—you get out there and start walking, girl! And don't let a little sweat bother you. I mean *glistening*.

Spiritual Satisfaction

One of the prevalent beliefs in our culture today is that most religions are essentially the same, and there are many paths all leading to God. Once again we must examine and hold on to the truth so we are not swept away by what sounds good. Ron Rhodes, president of Reasoning from the Scriptures ministries and professor at Dallas Theological Seminary, says this:

> The truth is, all religions are essentially different and only superficially the same. Some say all religions are similar because they all teach ethics. The truth is that the other world religions fundamentally seek to help bad people become better by choosing better personal ethics. Christianity, on the other hand, invites spiritually dead people to become spiritually alive.[3]

Ron adds,

> The various religions also teach different views of God. Jesus taught about a triune God (Matthew 28:19). Muhammad (the founder of Islam) taught that the one God is not a Trinity. Hinduism refers to many gods that are extensions of the one impersonal Brahman. Buddhism teaches that the concept of God is essentially irrelevant. Obviously, these religions are not pointing to the same God. If one is right, the others are wrong.[4]

As Christians, we believe what Jesus said was true. Jesus declared, "I am the way the truth and the life. No one comes to the Father except through me."[5] Just in case the Colossians were still wavering about who Jesus was, Paul went ahead and gave one more review lesson to make sure beyond a shadow of a doubt that they understood. (We can all use a little review lesson once in a while, can't we?)

Colossians 2:9-10

In Christ all the fullness of the Deity lives in bodily form, and you have been given fullness in Christ, who is the head over every power and authority.

Christ's deity is stated in no uncertain terms. Christ is God. As a reminder, the word "fullness" is *pleroma,* meaning the sum total of who God is and all of His being and attributes. Jesus and the Father are One. Jesus is not a god; He is The God. He is the head over every power and authority. We read this truth earlier in Colossians, but now Paul brings it into personal terms. *We* have been given fullness in Christ. Now the actual Greek word in this statement is not *pleroma*, but rather *pleroo*, which shares the same root but has a slightly different application. It means "to complete or satisfy or be filled."

Christ *completes* us. He is enough. He is our soul's satisfaction. In every human there is a hunger, a deep need for satisfaction and completeness. We try to find that satisfaction in all sorts of places. Success, popularity, marriage, divorce, charitable service, church work, hobbies, friends, children, accomplishments, diets, food, and substances of all kinds seem to call out to us, saying, "I'm satisfying. I will fulfill you." Yet they always leave us hungering for more, or something different or something better. Seventeenth-century mathematician, physicist, inventor, and philosopher Blaise Pascal described these longings and desires much more eloquently than I can. Here's what he wrote:

> What else does this craving, and this helplessness, proclaim but that there was once in man a true happiness, of which all that now remains is the empty print and trace? This he tries in vain to fill with everything around him, seeking in things that are not there the help he cannot find in those

that are, though none can help, since this infinite abyss
can be filled only with an infinite and immutable object;
in other words by God himself.[6]

Read his words several times and contemplate its truth. Our infinite longings can only be filled with one thing, and that is the infinite God. Christ in you, the hope of glory. Spiritually speaking, we need no other. There is nothing additional needed for salvation. And there is nothing additional needed for spiritual satisfaction. Feelings may sometimes fail us, making us think we need more. Remember the words of David, "The LORD is my shepherd, I have all that I need."[7] The power and presence of God dwells within you. He has set up residence there and our soul is satisfied.

Add-Ons

For about two weeks last year I became a bicycle enthusiast. My birthday just happened to be around that time, so I told my husband that all I wanted for my birthday was a bicycle. Just a simple bike I could ride on the bike trails around north Dallas was all I was asking for. Well, Curt has always been a wonderful gift giver, so when he went to shop for a bike to give me for my birthday he didn't go to Wal-Mart or a garage sale like I told him. No, he went to Big Bike City and found a good deal on a bike for me, but he didn't stop there. The bike experts helped him understand that if I was going to take up cycling (which I had every intention of doing—at least for a couple of weeks I did, I promise) I would need to have cycling outfits to wear. And don't forget the padded seat, and the helmet and the tire pump and bike lock and three-year warranty.

All I wanted was a bike, but I received so much more! I'm sure one day I really will get serious about cycling—but I am not wearing those skintight shorts, no way, nohow! Now if you think walking into Big Bike City (which is not their real name, by the way) will add on a lot of extras to a simple bike purchase, you should visit Colossae in Paul's day. Not for bikes (they hadn't been invented then) but for add-ons— religious add-ons. When someone became a Christian, they were told they needed to buy into additional religious stuff to make the package complete. Now remember, Paul had already told them they were complete in Christ, but now he gets specific.

First he addresses the Deluxe Judaizers Add-On Package, complete with circumcision and Jewish laws and ceremonies. Although you may read through this quickly, wondering, *What does circumcision have to do with me?* the truth is, this passage has a powerful proclamation of our salvation. Once we were dead, but now we are alive with Christ. Don't miss the beauty in the message that we could not save ourselves—instead, Christ paid our ransom on the cross, and by the power of God He rose from the dead. Paul is reminding the early Christians that the old covenant is gone and circumcision is obsolete.

COLOSSIANS 2:11-15

In him you were also circumcised, in the putting off of the sinful nature, not with a circumcision done by the hands of men but with the circumcision done by Christ, having been buried with him in baptism and raised with him through your faith in the power of God, who raised him from the dead. When you were dead in your sins and in the uncircumcision of your sinful nature, God made you alive with Christ. He forgave us all our sins, having canceled the written code, with its regulations, that was against us and that stood opposed to us; he took it away, nailing it to the cross. And having disarmed the powers and authorities, he made a public spectacle of them, triumphing over them by the cross.

The Gnostics had their own set of spiritual add-ons in the form of regulations, rules, and self-denials. Some of them added the worship of angels to the Super Deluxe Religious Experience Package deal. And of course the Judaizers wanted to add religious festivals and Sabbath days into the mix. It's easy to get caught up in man's rules and begin to think they make us more spiritual. Paul puts it out plain and clear:

COLOSSIANS 2:16-23

Therefore do not let anyone judge you by what you eat or drink, or with regard to a religious festival, a New Moon celebration or a Sabbath day. These are a shadow of the things that were to come; the

*reality, however, is found in Christ. Do not let anyone who delights
in false humility and the worship of angels disqualify you for the prize.
Such a person goes into great detail about what he has seen, and his
unspiritual mind puffs him up with idle notions. He has lost connection with the Head, from whom the whole body, supported and held
together by its ligaments and sinews, grows as God causes it to grow.*

*Since you died with Christ to the basic principles of this world, why,
as though you still belonged to it, do you submit to its rules: "Do not
handle! Do not taste! Do not touch!"? These are all destined to perish
with use, because they are based on human commands and teachings.
Such regulations indeed have an appearance of wisdom, with their self-
imposed worship, their false humility and their harsh treatment of the
body, but they lack any value in restraining sensual indulgence.*

In today's religious circles we still have voices trying to sell us religious add-ons. Some tell us what we ought to do and some tell us what
we ought not to do. These demanding voices try to make us feel less
spiritual if we do not comply or have the same type of religious experience. Often denominations and religious groups have good intentions
for additional rules and regulations, but they tend to deal with outward
behaviors and not the heart. We must be on our guard against becoming legalistic and missing the heart of what it means to live in Christ.
Theologian Charles Ryrie wrote, "What is legalism? It is a wrong attitude toward the code of laws under which a person lives...Thus legalism may be defined as 'a fleshly attitude which conforms to a code for
the purpose of exalting self.'"[8]

We must be cautious of those who put pressure on us to do something or not do something for the Lord, and we must remember that
we are complete in Christ and our salvation was taken care of on the
cross. Don't confuse obedience to Christ with legalism. Religious add-
ons and legalistic rules are made by man and tend to glorify self; obedience to Christ is living a life that glorifies Him according to Scripture.
We are missing the point of obedience if we are more concerned about
outward appearance than a person's heart. Paul hit the nail on the head
in his very last words in this section. He said of the rules and regulations

that "they lack any value" because they can't change a person's heart. We can do a lot of outward things that make us look good as Christians, but it's what is on the inside that counts. God looks not at the outward appearance but at the heart.

Confident Steps

ADDITIONAL READING: Galatians 5—Freedom in Christ

BATTLE FOR THE TRUTH:

Confidence Defeater—*I'm never good enough. I need to do more.*

Confidence Builder—We walk in confidence knowing we are complete in Christ, and our confidence is strengthened as we are rooted and built up in Him.

CHOICES:

- Walk with Christ—abide in Him throughout your day.
- Spend time with Christ in the secret place, meditating on His Word and praying.
- Be built up in Christ, finding your strength and approval in Him.
- Strengthen your faith through good Bible teaching.
- Overflow with thankfulness.
- Look to Christ alone for your soul's satisfaction.
- Beware of religious additions (add-ons) to salvation in Christ.

DELIBERATE PLAN: Power walk.

Walking and talking to the Lord can be a wonderful time not only to pray, but to listen. I want to encourage you to step outside and take a walk, just you and God. Now if it is the dead of winter then you may want to go to a local mall to do a little mall walking. As you walk, examine some of the aspects of walking with Christ that we talked about in this chapter. Are you rooted in Him, built up in Him, strengthened in your faith, and overflowing with thankfulness? Are you experiencing your soul's satisfaction in Him? Seek Him, and spend some time contemplating His presence in your life. Thank Him that He is Enough.

PART FOUR

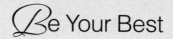 Be Your Best

*"Since we are surrounded by such
a great cloud of witnesses,
let us throw off everything that hinders
and the sin that so easily entangles,
and let us run with perseverance
the race marked out for us.
Let us fix our eyes on Jesus, the author
and perfecter of our faith,
who for the joy set before him endured the cross,
scorning its shame, and sat down at the right
hand of the throne of God.
Consider him who endured such opposition
from sinful men,
so that you will not grow weary and lose heart."*

HEBREWS 12:1-3

*"Life consists of melting illusions,
correcting mistakes and replacing outgrown clothing.
But, I remind myself, there is no other way to grow."*

A.P. GOUTHEY

CHAPTER SEVEN

Glorious Makeover

"One thing I do: Forgetting what is behind
and straining toward what is ahead,
I press on toward the goal to win the prize
for which God has called me
heavenward in Christ Jesus."

PHILIPPIANS 3:13-14

"Live near to God and all things will appear little to you
in comparison with eternal realities."

ROBERT MURRAY M'CHEYNE

Have you ever gotten one of those disastrous haircuts where you thought your life was completely over until your hair grew back? A number of years ago, I made the mistake of going to a new salon and telling the big, burly Turkish hairdresser I wanted to try a new, shorter style for my hair. Big Mistake! He started chopping and chopping, and before I could stop him, most of my hair was on the salon floor. I walked into the chop shop with long blond hair, and I walked out with short hair that was rather unbecoming.

When my friends saw me they typically said, "Oh, you got your hair cut. It'll grow back." That's never really good to hear. One bright-side note to the dismal hairdo was that as it began to grow back, it kind of started to resemble Princess Diana's haircut. Now in my whole life no one has ever told me I looked like Princess Di, except during the time when I had the new hairdo. I remember getting on an airplane and the male flight attendant exclaimed, "You look just like Lady Di! I'm going to call you Princess for the rest of the flight." And he did. It was a little eerie, to tell you the truth, but it was the only time in all my life that I came close to being princess for a day.

As little girls, didn't we all have that dream of being a princess? For me, I used to watch Cinderella and think how exciting it would be to have the prince pursue me, find me, and invite me to be his princess. Can you imagine the anticipation Cinderella must have felt after the prince found her? The glass shoe fit, and now she was going to live in the palace. No more rags, no more evil stepmother, no more endless chores. Wouldn't it be interesting if one of the versions of Cinderella would show us what is was like for her in the time between the fitting of the glass slipper and her wedding with the prince?

Talk about a transitional time in her life! She needed to change both her way of life and her way of thinking. She was no longer a slave girl, she was a princess. Her mind no doubt began to focus on different things—palace things, kingdom things. Her heart was set on a new love, love for her prince. With that one glass slipper, everything in her life would change from inside and out.

Like Cinderella, we too have been rescued from the dominion of darkness and have been invited to share in the inheritance of the kingdom of light. As believers in Christ, we have become citizens of a new kingdom, a heavenly one. But we are not there yet. We are daughters of the King, and we look forward in anticipation to the day we will enter the palace of heaven.

Seeking His Kingdom

Colossians seems to speak directly to this time of anticipation of the next kingdom. It's as if the King has given us instructions on how to prepare for the wedding between Christ and His church. Paul changed direction in his letter to the Colossians here. He switched the focus of the second half to how we can practically live out and apply the treasure of Christ to our own daily living. He started off by talking about the focus we should have as Christians.

COLOSSIANS 3:1-4

Since, then, you have been raised with Christ, set your hearts on things above, where Christ is seated at the right hand of God. Set your minds on things above, not on earthly things. For you died, and your life is now hidden with Christ in God. When Christ, who is your life, appears, then you also will appear with him in glory.

We have another kingdom for which we are destined! Our hearts and minds ought to be set on that kingdom, not this one. The phrase "set your hearts on things above" means "keep seeking the things above." It implies a continual, earnest seeking. In other words, don't stop seeking the treasures of God's kingdom. Now the challenge for us is that the things of *this* kingdom are so distracting. They shout at us, saying, "Look at me, focus on me, stress out about me." Our hearts weaken, and our desires fade for the palace that seems so far away as we become consumed with our temporary earthly stuff: our appearance, our possessions, our relationships.

In His sermon on the mount, Jesus talked about the worries and distractions of our world as compared to seeking His kingdom. Listen to the words of our Prince as He speaks to our hearts. Picture Him lovingly telling you these words as He reassuringly looks into your eyes:

That is why I tell you not to worry about everyday life—whether you have enough food and drink, or enough clothes to wear. Isn't life more than food, and your body more than clothing? Look at the birds. They don't plant or harvest or store food in barns, for your heavenly Father feeds them. And aren't you far more valuable to him than they are? Can all your worries add a single moment to your life?

And why worry about your clothing? Look at the lilies of the field and how they grow. They don't work or make their clothing, yet Solomon in all his glory was not dressed as beautifully as they are. And if God cares so wonderfully for wildflowers that are here today and thrown into the fire tomorrow, he will certainly care for you. Why do you have so little faith?

So don't worry about these things, saying, "What will we eat? What will we drink? What will we wear?" These things dominate the thoughts of unbelievers, but your heavenly Father already knows all your needs. Seek the Kingdom of God above all else, and live righteously, and he will give you everything you need.[1]

How tenderly and kindly the Lord takes care of our needs! When I change my focus to God's kingdom and seek Him above all else, my worries about the things here diminish. I need His help in setting my heart on things above.

> *Father, keep my heart set on Your kingdom. Help me not to get so distracted and worried with this one. Help me to rest in the assurance of Your power and strength. You are my Keeper. You know my needs, and You watch over Your children.*

Not only are we to set our hearts on things above, but that is where our mind should be as well. Our thinking as well as our affections ought to be pointed toward heaven. When a runner competes in a race, her focus needs to be on one thing and one thing only, the finish line. If a runner looks to the right or the left and gets distracted, then she loses the race. Our focus is important in the race of life as well. We must fill our minds with things that point us to eternity and prepare us for that kingdom. We must ask ourselves, "What do I typically fill my mind up with, and in what direction do those things point me?" The Scripture is not saying we should never look at a fashion or decorating magazine or a secular movie or television show. It's not telling us to neglect the kids and spend all our time praying and reading the Bible. It is telling us to consider our focus. Where are our attention and our affection?

Things Above

"Things above" sounds so nebulous. What are "things above"? Paul repeated the term twice, so he must have been serious about it. I know what things down here are. Jesus even named a few of them in the passage we just read, what we eat and drink and what we wear. We could add to that list where we live, what school our kids go to, what we will do with our time. None of these things are bad things, but they do not need to consume our focus. So what are heavenly things? The first heavenly thing that comes to mind is God Himself—Father, Son, and Spirit. Concentrating on things above means continually focusing on Him and His agenda, asking ourselves questions like, "What would God have me do in this situation?" "Would this please Him?" "What does He want to teach me here?"

Seeking God's kingdom means desiring to do what He wants me to do and desiring His will above my own. It's all about loving Him more and looking forward to His kingdom. Seeking things above does not mean halfhearted Christianity! Can you imagine Cinderella, as she was supposed to be preparing to go to the palace, just sitting around saying, "Oh well, I guess the prince is okay. I don't really know him that well. I have no idea how he wants me to dress or what he likes. I think I'll just stay busy around here. I wonder what some of my evil stepsisters are doing right now? I guess I'd better go find out." No, if I were Cinderella, I'd want to know what the prince is like. I'd study up on a little palace etiquette, how the king wants me to live and act, and I'd start getting rid of some of my old rags.

To passionately pursue "things above" means that we change our perspective from dwelling on the temporal to dwelling on the eternal. We begin to look at life from God's perspective and think about things in light of heaven. Colossians reminds us that we have died to the old self and our life is now hidden with Christ in God. We are alive in Christ and dead to the old sinful nature. I don't want us to miss the beauty in that phrase "hidden with Christ in God." We are safe in the arms of Christ. No one can snatch us out of His hands. We know that our eternal destiny is secure in Him. One day when Christ appears, then we will also appear with Him in glory. Oh, glorious day!

Glorious Day

My daughter Joy just got married to a wonderful young man. He was without a doubt Mr. Right. I can say that because his name is actually Adam Wright, but he really is Mr. Right also in every way. I always prayed for our daughters to marry men who love God, love His Word, love hard work, and love our daughters. Adam is really the answer to our prayers. As he and Joy planned their wedding, they didn't want to use a traditional wedding march, so they searched and searched for just the right song that would be meaningful and also make a great entrance song for when the doors fly open and the bride walks down the aisle.

They found an old hymn called "One Day." Several Christian artists have now created an updated version of this great old hymn, giving it an upbeat twist and a new name, "Glorious Day." The song is perfect because it talks about all Christ has done for us on the cross and the glorious day He rose from the dead. The song reaches a high point when it describes the glorious day when we will see Him face to face. The book of Revelation says that one day as believers in Christ we will participate in the marriage supper of the Lamb when the bride of Christ (the church) will be joined with Christ. A wedding here on earth is a wonderful picture of that glorious day when we will be with Christ up there.

Here are the words to the hymn written by J. Wilbur Chapman (1859–1918):

"One Day" ("Glorious Day")

One day when heaven was filled with His praises,
One day when sin was as black as could be,
Jesus came forth to be born of a virgin—
Dwelt among men, my example is He!

Refrain
Living, He loved me;
Dying, He saved me;
Buried, He carried my sins far away;
Rising, He justified freely forever:
One day He's coming—
Oh, glorious day!

One day they led Him up Calvary's mountain,
One day they nailed Him to die on the tree;
Suffering anguish, despised and rejected:
Bearing our sins, my Redeemer is He!

One day the grave could conceal Him no longer,
One day the stone rolled away from the door;
Then He arose, over death He had conquered;
Now is ascended, my Lord forevermore!

One day the trumpet will sound for His coming,
One day the skies with His glories will shine;
Wonderful day, my beloved ones bringing;
Glorious Savior, this Jesus is mine!

Refrain

Living, He loved me;
Dying, He saved me;
Buried, He carried my sins far away;
Rising, He justified freely forever
One day He's coming—
Oh, glorious day![2]

Is that great? They couldn't have picked a better song! Adam and Joy gave me strict instructions as to when I was supposed to stand. As you know, when the mother of the bride rises to her feet, then the audience follows suit, the doors are flung open, and there stands the bride. It was perfect! The doors flew open right when the music reached its height at "Oh, glorious day!" It was spectacular. I wish you could have been there. (I'm not *too* proud, am I?)

I tell you that story just to remind you of what we have to look forward to. We are living for that glorious day. Just as a bride prepares for and focuses on her wedding, so we prepare for and focus on that day. Although Joy and I tried to keep things in perspective, there were times when the planning and preparing for her wedding became all-consuming. We worked toward it, we prayed about it, we shopped for it, we thought about it all the time! As the bride of Christ, we His beloved are supposed to be completely consumed with our wedding day. We are to be thinking about it, planning for it, and preparing for it as our main focus in life, setting our hearts and minds on things above.

Not So Lovely

Imagine you are at a wedding. The processional plays, the brides-maids proceed down the aisle, and then the big moment everyone is waiting for—the doors fly open and there stands the bride! And she is dressed in rags—dirty, filthy rags. The crowd can't believe it. Isn't she the bride? Isn't she supposed to be in a wedding gown? Did she not have enough money to buy a new dress? No, the groom bought a beautiful dress for her. Then did she forget it was her wedding day? Or even worse yet, what if she simply didn't care?

Surely this would never happen, you say. Yet in regard to Christ and His bride (the church) this isn't such a far-fetched description. What kind of clothing are we wearing? Colossians tells us we must put off the rags of our old sinful nature and put on the beautiful new clothes of righteousness Christ has given us. It's tempting to put on some of those old, comfy, worn-out outfits, but they are no longer becoming to the child of a king. Just as Cinderella had to get rid of her old rags and prepare for her new life in the palace, so we must get rid of a few old habits and actions. Paul gives us a list of items to discard from the closets of our hearts:

COLOSSIANS 3:5-7

Put to death, therefore, whatever belongs to your earthly nature: sexual immorality, impurity, lust, evil desires and greed, which is idolatry. Because of these, the wrath of God is coming. You used to walk in these ways, in the life you once lived. But now you must rid yourselves of all such things as these: anger, rage, malice, slander, and filthy language from your lips. Do not lie to each other, since you have taken off your old self with its practices and have put on the new self, which is being renewed in knowledge in the image of its Creator. Here there is no Greek or Jew, circumcised or uncircumcised, barbarian, Scythian, slave or free, but Christ is all, and is in all.

Notice Paul says, "Put to death…" We are not supposed to let these old rags linger in our lives. Paul didn't want us to just put them in a box in our closet in case we want to pull them out again. We are supposed to put them to death. Get rid of them completely. Clean house!

These are ugly items that may have been in our life before Christ, but they just aren't the right outfit for us anymore as His bride. Paul says that since we have a new life in Christ, we have taken off the old life. The term "taken off" comes from a phrase meaning to divest or put off clothing. When we came to Christ we received a divine makeover—now why would we go back and wear all those outfits that are so unbecoming? They are certainly not our best look.

Let's examine the "must go" clothes that Paul identified in this closet cleanout:

Sexual immorality, impurity, lust. In his letter to the Ephesians Paul proclaimed the beauty of sexual purity: "For this reason a man will leave his father and mother and be united to his wife, and the two will become one flesh. This is a profound mystery—but I am talking about Christ and the church."[3] God intends for sexual relations to be between a man and wife in the context of marriage, because it is a picture of Christ and His church. The Greek word for sexual immorality is *porneia*, which refers to adultery, fornication, or illicit sexual intercourse. Paul warned the Corinthians, "Flee from sexual immorality. All other sins a man commits are outside his body, but he who sins sexually sins against his own body. Do you not know that your body is a temple of the Holy Spirit, who is in you, whom you have received from God? You are not your own, you were bought at a price. Therefore honor God with your body."[4]

Evil desires. This concept stresses the lust, craving, and longing we have for what is usually forbidden. It refers to the whole world of active lusts and an irrational longing for pleasure and unbridled desires. James talked about these evil desires when he wrote, "Each one is tempted when, by his own evil desire, he is dragged away and enticed. Then, after desire has conceived, it gives birth to sin and sin, when it is full-grown, gives birth to death."[5] Just as we are to love the Lord with all our hearts, we are also to guard our hearts from evil desires, for out of our hearts come the wellsprings of life. Do not let unbridled cravings and longings take over your heart.

Greed. Paul said that greed was idolatry. Idolatry is worshiping anything other than God. Typically we think of greed in terms of money, yet greed can encompass other areas we wholeheartedly pursue, hoping they will satisfy us. Success, fame, food, approval, status, power, and people all can become idols in our lives. Typically we don't think of ourselves as idol worshipers, but idols can overtake our hearts easily and without notice. In his book *Counterfeit Gods*, author Timothy Keller writes, "The human heart takes good things like a successful career, love, material possessions, even family, and turns them into ultimate things. Our hearts deify them as the center of our lives because we think they can give us significance and security, safety and fulfillment, if we attain them."[6] May God open our eyes to the deep idols of our hearts.

Anger, rage. Anger in and of itself is an emotion we feel when we sense an injustice has taken place, whether toward us or someone else. Paul cautions in his letter to the Ephesians, "In your anger do not sin." We may feel a genuine anger, but we must be careful not to sin with that anger. Paul advised to not let the sun go down on your anger. He went on to say, "Do not let any unwholesome talk come out of your mouths...get rid of all bitterness, rage and anger, brawling and slander."[7] When we let anger fester and grow, it develops into bitterness and unforgiveness and eventually explodes like a volcano, destroying everything in its path. So the solution is to deal with our anger in a wise and thoughtful way. Forgiving, gently confronting, speaking the truth in love and communicating with kindness, all allow anger to subside with positive results.

Rage is an unhealthy outburst of anger. When we have not dealt with our anger properly through positive paths, rage takes us down a different and unproductive road. Rage is a destructive outburst that not only is unbecoming of Christ's bride, but can destroy relationships and deeply hurt tender hearts. Self-control is a beautiful fruit of God's Spirit and much lovelier clothing for a lady.

Malice, slander. Malice means the deliberate intention to hurt or bring destruction on another person. It goes hand in hand with slander—trying to hurt someone or destroy them with your words. In Romans we read,

> *Love must be sincere. Hate what is evil; cling to what is good. Be devoted to one another in brotherly love. Honor one another above yourselves...*
>
> *Do not repay anyone evil for evil. Be careful to do what is right in the eyes of everybody. If it is possible, as far as it depends on you, live at peace with everyone. Do not take revenge, my friends, but leave room for God's wrath, for it is written: "It is mine to avenge; I will repay," says the Lord. On the contrary: "If your enemy is hungry, feed him; if he is thirsty, give him something to drink. In doing this, you will heap burning coals on his head." Do not be overcome by evil, but overcome evil with good.* [8]

Filthy language from your mouth. Our words reveal what is in our heart. Filthy language refers to vile communication and includes every kind of foul-mouthed abusiveness as well as the obvious offensive words. It's an outbreak of a loveless, disrespectful, or uncaring spirit toward another person. Let's clean up our mouths by first cleaning up our hearts and minds. Jesus said, "Out of the overflow of the heart, the mouth speaks. The good man brings good things out of the good stored up in him, and the evil man brings evil things out of the evil stored up in him."[9] We need to be aware of some of the influences in our lives that make us familiar with filthy language, and instead fill our minds and ears with good words. Let's ask the Lord to clean up our hearts and fill them with love and respect toward the people around us.

Do not lie to each other. Honesty and integrity are two attributes we must wear in every area of our lives. We are to take off the ugly rags of deceit and deception. There are many cultures in today's world that do not value speaking the truth. We must not live like the world, for we are different—we are Christ's bride. We have taken off the clothing that the world wears and have put on new clothing. Consider your relationships and what comes out of your mouth when you are telling a story about someone else. Guard your mouth. Lean on God, not on deceit, to lead you where you want to go. Speak the truth, and be sure to do it in love. Don't use truth as an excuse to gossip either. Just because you know someone else's story doesn't mean you need to share it, even if it is true. Bottom line—be careful what you let emerge from your lips. Dishonesty disrupts the unity of the body and destroys your reputation in the process.

New and Renewed

It feels good to clean out my closet and get rid of some of the outfits that are outdated and just don't look good on me. Spiritually speaking, it feels good to get rid of some of the old garments of our sinful nature. Our old, ugly clothes could have been a wardrobe of anything from filthy language to sexual immorality. We have been made new in Christ. We are learning and growing every day in Him, and we are being refashioned into His image. Paul says we are renewed in knowledge in the image of our Creator. The more we know Him, the more we become like Him. And might I add, the new you is a lovely you! A new confidence, a God-confidence, develops as you discard your old, ugly clothes.

God doesn't want us to get rid of them because He is mean and uncaring. Quite the contrary—because of His love for us He doesn't want us to get tangled up in behaviors that can lead us toward ruin and destruction in our lives. I was thinking about this the other day as I was walking my dogs. When it is snake season, I don't let my dogs go down near the creek because there are water moccasins in the area. I steer my dogs clear of the high grass where they could get bitten by a snake. Now it's tempting for them, and they want to run down near the creek, but I know what is best for them. If they listen to me, they will enjoy a life free of snakebites. Do you see what I'm saying? It is out of love that I keep them from the high grass near the creek, and it is out of love that God steers us clear of harmful behaviors.

Janeé is a beautiful and confident sister in Christ, but she wasn't always that way. From childhood she carried around the ugly baggage of deception, and she dragged that bag along through early adulthood. As a young girl she was sexually abused by a neighbor, and she began covering it up by telling stories. Her stories grew as she entered college, with the purpose of making people think she was something she was not. Her lying became more intense as she struggled with an eating disorder, to the point that she told people she had cancer instead of letting them know the truth. When she entered the career world, she lied about her age and background. She thought she was doing pretty well at juggling all the stories and deceit.

One day she was asked to speak to a group of young ladies on the topic of etiquette and beauty. Yet when she arrived to speak she realized her audience needed to talk about deeper issues. As she saw the needs in these young girls, she became convicted of her own need. The Lord began to work on Janeé's heart and drew her to Himself. She made a decision to place her faith in Christ and follow Him. As she grew to know and love Christ, she also realized He had freed her from the need to tell lies. She knew the deception was part of her old wardrobe and it was time to get rid of all those ugly rags. She came clean and confessed to her family and friends that she had been living a lie.

It wasn't easy, but Janeé knew that deception certainly did not fit in her new wardrobe, which was being renewed in knowledge of the image of her Creator. She is now a new woman. She is a confident woman, not hiding under a covering of lies to make her look good and get her where she wants to go. She is a radiant woman who depends on Christ, and He is her covering. Getting rid of old, unbecoming, sinful behavior was an important step for Janeé in living a confident life. She knows that Christ has made her new and has equipped her with gifts and talents to serve Him. In fact, she has now started a television show that encourages women to be real and authentic.[10] What lovely qualities for a woman who finds her identity in Christ! As Paul said at the close of this passage, "Christ is all and is in all." That's how Janeé defines her life now, and we can do the same.

Confident Steps

ADDITIONAL READING: 2 Corinthians 5 and 6—Looking forward to heaven

BATTLE FOR THE TRUTH:

Confidence Defeater—*God doesn't understand me. He couldn't love me.*

Confidence Builder—God loves us and knows that a beautiful confidence awakens in us as we set our affection on His kingdom and get rid of unbecoming behaviors.

CHOICES:

- Keep seeking the things of God's kingdom.
- Recognize as a follower of Christ that you are His bride.
- Put off whatever belongs to your earthly nature.
- Flee sexual immorality.
- Examine your heart concerning idols.
- Rid yourself of anger, rage, malice, filthy language.
- Do not lie to each other.
- Continue to grow in knowledge of Him.
- Honor Christ as all, and recognize He is in all.

DELIBERATE PLAN: Check your closet.

In this chapter we learned about behaviors, actions, and attitudes that are unbecoming to the bride of Christ. Now it is time to do a little closet cleanout. It's not always easy, but we must ask the Lord to help us and gently convict us of areas in our lives where things need to be discarded. Look back over the list of items Paul tells us to put off and see if any are present in your life. Listen to the Holy Spirit's gentle voice, not of guilt but of conviction. Ask for God's help in getting rid of some of those ugly outfits. Just like we may want to have a friend come over to help us clean out our closets and figure out what clothes need to be tossed, so too you may want to consider asking a godly friend to help you and hold you accountable.

CHAPTER EIGHT

ou Look Divine!

> *"She is clothed with strength and dignity;*
> *She can laugh at the days to come.*
> *She speaks with wisdom,*
> *And faithful instruction is on her tongue."*
>
> PROVERBS 31:25-26

> *"There is a beauty in holiness as well*
> *as a beauty of holiness."*
>
> GEORGE SWINNOCK

One Sunday not too long ago, Curt and I went out after church to eat at one of our favorite little diners. It's the kind of place where you pay at the cash register when you leave, and you never know who you are going to meet as you wait in line. On this particular Sunday, a beautiful woman with true Southern belle charm came up behind us, and I'm glad she did! The first thing she said to me was, "Sugar, that dress looks fabulous on you!"

As you can imagine, I immediately liked this woman. She went on to say in the deepest South Carolina drawl you can imagine, "I grew up in a family with for-ah sis-tas (translation, *four sisters*), and our mamma always told us it doesn't matter where you buy an outfit or if it is the latest style. What matters most is that the color is *your* color and the style flatters *your* figure. Mamma told us, don't wear anything that doesn't flatter you to pieces."

Then she added, "And honey, your dress flatters you to pieces."

Well, sugar, I want you to know I was walking a little more tall and confident the rest of that day. I'll probably wear that dress to every special occasion for the next ten years! Have you ever discovered one of those perfect outfits that is just right for you? Right color, right style, the kind in which you feel like a million bucks even if you did get it on sale at Ross Dress for Less. You know when you find it, because everyone tells you how great you look in it.

Spiritually speaking, God has the perfect outfit for us. It's actually quite flattering. Not for our glory, but for His. Yet it sure makes us look lovely as well. When we wear this outfit we can walk in great confidence, knowing we are in the finest apparel created by the Ultimate Designer. This Designer knows what looks best on us, and you never need to doubt His wisdom. When you wear this clothing you not only look good, but you make other people look good. You feel a deep sense of joy. If you ever thought clothing was the key to your confidence, you are right—spiritual clothing, that is! Let's take a look at the flattering outfit He has designed for us. And keep in mind He has already paid for it.

Colossians 3:12-13

As God's chosen people, holy and dearly loved, clothe yourselves with compassion, kindness, humility, gentleness and patience. Bear with each other and forgive whatever grievances you may have against one another. Forgive as the Lord forgave you.

We should pay close attention to the way Paul begins this section. He begins by describing believers in Christ as God's chosen people, holy and dearly loved. What a perfect way for a groom to address his bride. Can you hear Jesus' voice saying this to you? "My precious one, I have chosen you. You are My beloved. My holy one, set apart just for Me. Here is your bridal gown. Here is how I want you to dress. I've paid for it with My own blood. I give you this clothing because I love you and I want the best for you. I ask you to wear it because you love Me too."

Beautiful Bride

The term the apostle Paul uses in Colossians 3:12 for "clothe yourself" is actually the Greek word *enduo,* which literally means to sink into a garment. As women we can understand that concept, can't we? I'm sure you have had the experience when you tried on several outfits, but then you slipped into that one perfect jacket or dress and said, "Ahh, this is it." You knew the outfit had found the perfect owner! Paul says, because you are holy and dearly loved, "sink into" these new clothes. We begin quite literally by sinking our arms into the first two qualities he mentions.

Compassion and kindness. When I think of these two qualities I think of arms reaching out to touch others in need. These are not passive words but proactive ones, as we must take the initiative to look for opportunities to show kindness and compassion. Who has God put into your path? How are you equipped to meet others' needs? You can't do everything, but you can do something. It begins with a caring heart, looking for places where you can use your gifts and talents to bless others. Ask the Lord to open your eyes to the needs around you, beginning with hearts that are hurting closest to you. Ultimately the greatest need anyone can have is their need for a savior. May our compassion extend to share Christ with those in need.

Kindness goes beyond actions; it ought to be found in our words as well. Proverbs 31 describes the godly wife as one who has the "law of kindness on her tongue." In other words her words are ruled by kindness. Don't be kind to people just to their face, be kind to them behind their back. That's true nobility and graciousness. Sometimes people's words don't match their actions. I've seen women who serve, serve, serve helping the homeless and down and out, yet with their tongues they can slice someone to shreds or make fun of them behind their back. When we tear other people down, we actually die inside, losing confidence and a sense of personal integrity. Be consistent with kind words and kind actions.

God will lead you to where you should serve. Just ask Him. About two years ago I was praying for the Lord to show me someplace new to serve. I personally love working with special-needs people, but I wasn't sure where or how to jump in. One Saturday I remember specifically praying that the Lord would direct my path, and all of a sudden the Joni and Friends ministry came to mind. I was familiar with it from a distance, and I knew they ministered to the needs of special-needs people in a variety of ways. Still, I didn't know if they had any contacts in Dallas or how I could get involved. So I asked the Lord if He would show me what to do. The next evening, Curt and I attended a large dinner function at a friend's home. As we were in the buffet line I started up a conversation with a delightful girl in front of me named Janet. When I asked her what she did, she said, "Oh, I work with Joni and Friends. Have you ever heard of them?" Janet and I became fast friends, and she helped me find ways I could serve the ministry using my gifts and talents.

Humility. Humility is a strong and beautiful quality. Jesus gave us the perfect picture of what humility looks like. He, being in very nature God, did not consider equality with God something to cling to. Instead, He gave up His heavenly rights and came to earth as a servant. He glorified God and thought of others before Himself. Humility doesn't mean you are a doormat, letting people walk all over you. Humility doesn't mean hating yourself or beating yourself up in your mind. Humility means being like Christ—looking up to God and looking out to the needs of others, but not looking at our own glory. Humility also means recognizing that all we have comes from Him. It means taking our cares to God, because we know we cannot handle everything on our own.

The bold and confident apostle Peter also mentioned putting on the clothing of humility. Look at how he encouraged us to be humble: "Clothe yourselves with humility toward one another, because, 'God opposes the proud but gives grace to the humble.' And God will exalt you in due time, if you humble yourselves under his mighty hand by casting all your cares on him because he cares for you."[1] We are never so prideful as when we say, "I can do this myself." We live humbly when we say, "Lord God, I know I need You in this hour. You know what I need. Thank You for caring for me and equipping me." Humility is a lovely piece of clothing on a confident woman, because she recognizes her dependence on God, and she looks out for the interests of others.

Gentleness. Gentleness is another one of those traits that may seem wimpy in today's world, yet it takes God's power and self-control to be gentle, especially in disagreeable circumstances. Paul warned the Philippians, "Let your gentleness be evident to all. The Lord is near." Anybody can lose their temper, yell, scream, and demean people. That's easy. It takes a person under God's control to handle things gently, and oh—how much more is accomplished through gentle means than strife! I want to encourage you to be gentle, beginning with those in your own home. Harsh words breed only harsh responses. Let your gentleness be evident to all because God is close by. He is gentle, gracious, full of loving kindness. Look to Him, asking Him to give you His gentleness as you relate with family members and those with whom you are associated.

Patience. Long-suffering is another word for patience. Are you willing to suffer long? In today's culture everything is fast. Patience seems to work against the grain of our fast-paced world, yet patience is something God has toward us. I'm so glad God doesn't look at us and say, "Why haven't you learned yet? How long will it take you to grow up?" The Bible tells us, "The Lord is compassionate and gracious, slow to anger, abounding in love."[2] The Bible says one of the fruits of God's spirit is patience.[3]

We need His patience, don't we? I'm not talking about having patience in the McDonald's drive-thru line. I'm talking about patience with our family and friends—having a gracious understanding and forgiveness toward them. The opposite of patience toward others would be resentment, wrath, or trying to get revenge. Are you patient to wait on God's timing? Are you patient toward others, recognizing we are all works in progress? We need to have the same sort of patience we hope other people will have toward us as. And remember, love is patient, love is kind.

Tender Mercies

In 1983, Robert Duvall and Tess Harper starred in a movie called *Tender Mercies*. Duvall played a former country-and-western music icon (Mac Sledge) who had become a penniless alcoholic. He offered to work at a rural Texas motel for room and board. Tess Harper played a young widow (Rosa Lee) of a Vietnam veteran who ran the motel with her son. As months passed, the former singer developed a bond with the woman and her son as he experienced the healing effects of her beautiful Christian compassion. Eventually they married as he began to rebuild his life. Despite his challenges and rough exterior, Rosa chose not to be demanding of him. She never threatened him, but rather gently, quietly, patiently—with tender mercies—trusted God to deal with her husband. She knew it was God's work, not hers.

The story came to a climax when Mac, in the midst of depression and confusion, drove away in his pickup, bought a bottle of alcohol, and considered leaving. Rosa waited in her bed, quoting Scripture to encourage herself as he left. Finally he came back to the house and reported, "I bought a bottle, but I poured it out. I didn't drink anything." Her tender mercies toward Mac helped him turn the corner in his life and come back to his family. He also eventually returned to the work he loved in songwriting.

Tender mercies—that's the beauty of God's love toward us. It's God's kindness that leads us to repentance. When we truly understand God's tender mercies toward us in His patience, compassion, love, and forgiveness, we are much more able to reflect tender mercies toward others. Rosa trusted God and reflected His kindness and compassion in her home. God used her gentle strength to change the life of her husband. Oh, the power of God's mercy and love when it is reflected in our lives!

Bear with one another…forgive as the Lord has forgiven you. Patience goes into bearing with someone. What does it mean to "bear with" someone? It means to persevere, to be patient with them, understanding that God is continuing to cause them to mature and help them grow. Whether it is a difficult child, a challenging roommate, a frustrating spouse, an annoying co-worker, or a very different fellow church member, we are called to bear with one another. In this, we may need to set boundaries, and we may need to confront in a loving manner. All relationships are difficult at times, and all take a bit of perseverance and dying to our own demands at times. Who do you need to bear with right now in your life?

As we bear with others, we must also continually forgive. And I said *must*. As Christians we are commanded throughout Scripture to forgive as we have been forgiven. Forgiveness doesn't mean you allow someone to continually walk all over you. No, we may need to set boundaries or communicate our concerns, but forgiveness means we give up our right to hold an offense against another person. It's a heart issue. And it is for your benefit much more than the offender's benefit. There are consequences with the law and with natural circumstances to be sure, yet forgiveness deals with the heart—it is a releasing of our mental grip of the offense. Jesus gave us the prime example when He hung on the cross and prayed, "Father, forgive them for they know not what they do."

Jesus also taught on the topic of forgiveness. When Peter asked Him how many times we should forgive our brother who has offended us, Peter thought he was extending great generosity by suggesting seven times. But Jesus took forgiveness further. He said we should forgive seventy times seven—which meant keep going and continually forgive. Then Jesus shared the story of the unforgiving servant. He had been forgiven of a great sum by his master, yet he would not forgive the little that was owed to him. Upon hearing of the unforgiving servant's deeds, the master sent him to be punished in prison until he could pay his debt. Jesus added, "This is how My heavenly Father will treat each of you unless you forgive your brother from your heart." Jesus was serious about forgiveness, and we must be too.

Do not take it lightly if you are holding onto unforgiveness. It is time to deal with it. If you want to walk in confidence, then you must forgive those who have offended you. I'm not saying it is easy. You may need to ask the great God, the one who forgives all your debt, to help you release the right to hold an offense over another person. Ask God to help you heal from your pain, and make an intentional effort to stop replaying the hurt in your mind. God is really good at forgiving. He can give you the strength and the desire to do it. Call on Him.

Completing the Outfit

We have a shoe place in Dallas where you can buy all sorts of fun and unique shoes for very low prices. The thing I like about going there is that the store is owned by Christians and they play Christian music throughout the store. (It sure is nice to shop for shoes while listening to Michael W. Smith or Casting Crowns.) At the encouragement of my daughters, I've stepped out of my comfort zone and purchased a few pairs of pumps with a little pizzazz. They insisted that the animal print stilettos would simply "make an outfit." Sure enough, whenever I wear a black skirt and top, those shoes bring it all together. Truly, the right shoes complete the outfit. The down side is that those shoes aren't exactly the most comfortable ones around.

Perhaps you've heard the phrase, "Beauty is pain." Looking your best is not always easy. Loving your best isn't always easy either. Paul told us that the way to tie the whole outfit together is through love. Here's how he put it:

COLOSSIANS 3:14

Over all these virtues put on love, which binds them all together in perfect unity.

Just like the perfect pair of shoes pulls an outfit together, so love pulls all the other qualities together. In his first letter to the Corinthians, Paul provided a "true love" description: "Love is patient, love is kind. It does not envy, it does not boast, it is not proud. It is not rude, it is not self-seeking, it is not easily angered, it keeps no record of wrongs. Love does not delight in evil but rejoices with the truth. It always protects, always trusts, always

10/23/2012

Title: Mistress of Rome
Item ID: 39550004434196
Due: 10/23/2012

Title: A woman's secret for
Item ID: 39550004642376
Due: 10/23/2012

Title: Thor [videorecording
Item ID: 39550004645155
Due: 9/26/2012

Westfield Memorial Library

9/25/2012 1:31:33 PM   908 789 4090

****

Roxanne Paylago

Title: A passion for vegeta

Item ID: 39550003371423

hopes, always perseveres. Love never fails."[4] That's how *my* love looks toward others—doesn't yours? Well, maybe not so much. I kind of fell short when he said, "Love is patient, love is kind"...and let's just skip over the part that says, "not easily angered." Needless to say, loving others goes way beyond sending someone a Happy Valentine's Day card.

Notice that the qualities in the description of love are qualities we have already talked about. Love is a dying to self, a giving to others, a thinking of others before ourselves. It is not being proud (humility). It isn't rude (gentleness); it perseveres (bears with others). Do you see how true love encompasses all of the other pieces of clothing? We must learn to walk in love, not by our own strength and power, but God's. When I look at Paul's definition of love, I see a picture of God's perfect love toward us. He is patient and kind, and He is not easily angered toward us. Maybe that is why Paul started off this entire section by reminding us that we are dearly loved. When we recognize how dearly loved we are by the Father, we walk in confidence and forgiveness. Knowing we are deeply loved gives us the power to love.

The Bible reminds us that God is love. We can go to Him, seeking His help to sincerely love others. It may not always feel warm and fuzzy. We may need to die to our own demands sometimes. But love is what truly pulls together the outfit. Will you choose to walk in love, even if it isn't easy?

> *Father, pour Your powerful love through us and touch the people You have placed in my life. Allow me to be a vessel to show this world what godly love looks like. Shine Your light brightly through me and beyond me. Touch others' lives through the love You show through me. In Jesus' name.*

Who Referees Your Heart?

As I am writing this book, the World Cup soccer matches are being played in South Africa. It is amazing to watch these world-class teams coming together on the field and playing with such agility and action. It's great to watch the games and cheer on your country, but can you imagine what it would be like to watch the soccer games if there were no referees helping to keep the game in order? It would be chaos. It wouldn't be the World Cup games any longer—it would be the World War games. Referees are vital to the game because they maintain order, call the penalties, and make sure the score is accurate.

Paul reminds us that we need a referee for our hearts as well. Fears, worries, disappointments, discouragements, anger, and frustrations can cause a riot in our hearts. We need the peace that only Christ can give to rule our hearts. Paul used a term which literally means referee or umpire, when he wrote:

Colossians 3:15-16

Let the peace of Christ rule in your hearts, since as members of one body you were called to peace. And be thankful. Let the word of Christ dwell in you richly as you teach and admonish one another with all wisdom, and as you sing psalms, hymns and spiritual songs with gratitude in your hearts to God.

When your day turns out badly or you feel overwhelmed at work, let the peace of Christ referee your heart. When a friend hurts you or your husband doesn't agree with you, let the peace of Christ umpire your heart. When the cancer diagnosis is confirmed or your son is rebelling or your husband just got laid off, let the peace that only Christ can bring rule your heart. How do we let Him referee? We begin by taking our eyes off of the situation and putting them on the Lord. As we look to the Lord and pour our hearts out to Him, we can praise Him for His sovereignty and the fact that He holds all things together. Thank Him for His love. We can ask for His help, comfort, and guidance. We give the situation over to Him and trust Him with our worries and what-ifs.

Just as a soccer player must acquiesce to the referee's decisions and leadership, we too must relinquish our desire to control the outcome. Recognizing that we are in good hands and can trust God's care, we can experience peace. This peace leads to peace with others as well. Peace within the body of Christ begins with peace in our own hearts. Paul said we are called to peace, and certainly the body of Christ is called to be peaceful with each other. Notice that Paul adds the phrase "And be thankful." When we are looking to God in thankfulness, we recognize His kind hand and we experience a deeper peace. (As we progress along, I want you to see how many times Paul mentions to be thankful.)

The more I know God's Word, the more I have a peace and comfort that He is in control. The more I memorize God's Word, the more the reassurance of His presence stays with me throughout my day. The more I meditate on God's Word, the more I think about God and set my heart and mind on things above. Paul told the Colossians to let the word of Christ dwell in them richly. Notice how he talked about the peace of Christ and now he talks about the word of Christ. Christ is all and is in all. The word of Christ, the Bible, ought to take up residence in our hearts, minds, and lives. Paul says it should live in our lives *richly*, like an honored guest. The opposite would be allowing the Word of God to dwell in our lives poorly or meagerly. Unfortunately, that seems to be the sad state of many Christians.

How well do you know the word of Christ? We must know the Bible and study it for ourselves so we know the truth about who God is and how He wants us to live. We need to know the truth if someone makes a claim about Christ, or we at least need to know how to find out. If you aren't already, I want to encourage you to get serious about knowing what the Bible says. You may want to join a Bible study at your church or start one at your workplace. Memorizing God's Word is also a way to let His word dwell in you richly.

Our confidence in God grows as we read about creation, or about how God led the Israelites out of Egypt and into the Promised Land. We learn to trust His power as we study about Jesus calming the sea or Daniel in the lion's den or Lazarus rising from the dead. We recognize that God is able to do all things when we see He fed the five thousand with five loaves of bread and two fish, and we are reminded that He can take what little we have to offer and do great things. We develop wisdom and desire righteousness as a result of letting the word of Christ dwell in us richly. Let's be wealthy when it comes to a knowledge of His Word!

One of the ways we allow His Word to dwell in us is through music. Now, as I alluded to earlier, I love Christian music. It feeds my soul with the good truth of God's Word, and it always points me back to Him. I remember a particular time when I was going to speak at a large conference with several other women who are incredibly polished speakers. I was especially uneasy because the old speaking fears popped back in my head. The morning of the conference, as I left my hotel and got into my car, I turned on my radio. A song was playing, "The Voice of Truth," sung by Casting Crowns. The song talks about facing your fears and having the faith to step out of the boat like Peter, and the faith to face the giant like David. I needed to hear that song right then and there! It ministered to me using the truths of God's Word, and I had the confidence to go on—a God-confidence, that is.

Pay attention to some of the old hymns, which are rich with truth. Some churches no longer sing hymns, or they may sing them in updated versions. A couple of years ago I bought a hymnal at a Christian bookstore, and now and then I enjoy refreshing my heart with some of the songs I sang as a young girl. Music feeds the spirit. Nourish your spirit with songs and hymns and spiritual songs. Oh—and did you notice that Paul said to enjoy this music with gratitude in your hearts toward God? Paul just can't stop being thankful!

Honor the Family Name

Did you grow up in a small town? I always wondered what that would have been like, since I always lived in big towns like Akron, Detroit, and Dallas. I do know that one of the negatives to living in a small town is that everyone knows your name. They know your family name. I wouldn't want to be in your shoes if you dishonored the family name. I can just picture Pa saying as you walk out the door to go meet your friends, "Remember who you belong to." A name is important, and to dishonor it brings shame on the whole family.

As followers of Christ, we have a new name. We bear the name of Christ. We must honor His name in what we say and do. Paul wrote,

COLOSSIANS 3:17

And whatever you do, whether in word or deed, do it all in the name of
the Lord Jesus, giving thanks to God the Father through him.

Our words and actions need to be consistent with the name we bear. If we say we are a follower of Christ yet gossip and tear down another person, then we are not reflecting the image of Christ. If we call ourselves His child and yet we speak hatefully to our neighbor, we are not bringing honor to His name. If we bear the name of Christ, then we need to act with integrity and live a life that pleases Him. Doing all in the name of Christ may mean that we act a little differently or talk a little differently than those who do not know Him.

Recently I wanted to illustrate this point at a Bible study for working women. So I went to Goodwill and found a shirt with a logo on it. It had obviously been worn by an employee or sales representative of a telecommunications group. I put it on and told the ladies that if I were an employee of this company, wearing this shirt, I would be expected to live up to the standards of the company. I would need to watch what I said and did because as a representative of the company, I would want to uphold their good name. In the same way, I want to live in a way that honors Christ in everything I say and do.

If we clothe ourselves with kindness, compassion, humility, gentleness, and patience, and complete the outfit with love, then we will most certainly honor Christ. If God's peace referees our heart, we will demonstrate the strength of Christ in our lives. If God's Word dwells in us richly our words will be filled with His truth. Let others see Jesus in everything you do and say. And by the way, did you see Paul's last phrase? "Giving thanks to God the Father." The guy just won't let up on this thankfulness business, will he? Maybe we should never stop as well!

Confident Steps

ADDITIONAL READING: Proverbs 31—A portrait of a lovely woman

BATTLE FOR THE TRUTH:

Confidence Defeater—*I am not pretty. No one notices me.*

Confidence Builder—Our true beauty and confidence

comes from living a life that honors Christ, allowing His love to shine brightly through us as we touch others.

CHOICES:

- Sink into the lovely outfit of the beautiful qualities Christ has given you.
- Reach out in compassion and kindness.
- Live with a humble heart.
- Bear with each other. Forgive as the Lord forgave you.
- Put on love to complete the outfit.
- Let the peace of Christ referee in your heart.
- Meditate, memorize, and study God's Word.
- Give thanks continually.
- Whatever you do or say, do all in the name of the Lord Jesus, honoring Him.

DELIBERATE PLAN: Wealthy in God's Word.

Set aside a little time each day to read the Bible on your own. I use the *One Year Bible*, which gives a reading from the Old Testament, the New Testament, and Psalms and Proverbs for each day. By the end of the year I have read the entire Bible. You can purchase it online and at most bookstores. Often on Sunday afternoons, I will take some time alone to meditate on certain passages. I go beyond reading to concentrate on what God is saying in His Word and to also consider what He is specifically telling me through it. Be intentional about growing rich in God's Word.

PART FIVE

Strengthen Your Relationships

*"Love must be sincere.
Hate what is evil; cling to what is good.
Be devoted to one another in brotherly love.
Honor one another above yourselves."*

ROMANS 12:9-10

*"Warmth, kindness, and friendship
are the most yearned for commodities in the world.
The person who can provide them will never be lonely."*

ANN LANDERS

$\mathscr{H}$ow to Live with Those Closest to You

"Submit to one another out of reverence for Christ."
Ephesians 5:21

*"The real test of your Christianity is not
how pious you look at the Lord's table on Sunday,
but how you act at the breakfast table at home."*
Vance Havner

Imagine for a moment you are a news reporter on the front lines of a war zone. Your job is to interview some of the officers to find out about how things are going in combat and learn about the morale of the military men and women. You find a lieutenant and pull him aside for an interview. You begin with the typical questions, "Where are you from? How long have you been in the military? Do you have family back home?" Then you decide to inquire about his commanding officer, so you ask, "What is your opinion of your captain for this unit?" You can hardly believe the answer. In fact, the lieutenant's answer makes you want to get out of that zone as soon as possible and run for safety.

Did he say the captain was an enemy informant or a terrible tyrant? No, he begins by saying, "I like the captain. I just don't agree with everything he says. He has a different way of doing things than I do, and honestly I could run this unit a whole lot better than he does. Actually—off the record here—I choose to do my own thing and ignore his orders."

As you recover from your shock, you ask him, "Okay, I get the fact that you don't exactly agree with the captain, but aren't you supposed to follow the chain of command? Do you follow his leadership when you go into battle?" The lieutenant answers, "Are you kidding, why would I follow him? When we go into battle, I do what I want. I'm a smart guy and I know how things should run here."

Now you're concerned and very curious about the safety of everyone on the front lines. You inquire, "Doesn't this cause problems on the battlefield with the men and women under you?" The lieutenant answers, "Yeah, it's a bit confusing. Since I don't follow the captain, the troops under me don't know who to follow, so yeah—it gets a little confusing and chaotic out there. But that's not really my fault. The general shouldn't have put the captain in that position. I'd do such a better job of leading this unit." Now you begin to edge away because you can't even imagine how this guy has survived the battles thus far, and you know for sure you don't want to be around for the next one. As you leave you ask a parting question. "So what do you think about the general?"

The lieutenant replies, "I like the general. I don't like the fact that he wants me to be subject to the captain, but other than that I really like the general."

That's probably the nuttiest war story you have ever heard, am I correct? Somehow that lieutenant missed the whole lesson on chain of command and order in the military. Order is vital for the military to run smoothly, productively, and safely. I'm thankful that story doesn't reflect how our armed forces actually run. I'm also thankful that our God is a God of order. We see the benefit of His design for order in every area of life: in corporations, in school systems, in the city governments, in the judicial system, and in home life. If there is not a plan for leadership in a community, then eventually disorder and chaos erupt.

Rules of Order

If you have ever been a part of a club or organization or have served on a board, then you are familiar with *Robert's Rules of Order*. First published in 1876, it has been the accepted set of guidelines for how to properly run a meeting for generations. It provides the proper protocol for everything from how to vote on a proposed idea to how to adjourn a meeting. I've been in many a meeting where we have referred back to *Robert's Rules of Order* so we would be assured of maintaining order in the meeting and providing structure for the future of the organization. Simply put, the rules of order help us run a meeting smoothly and wisely. It is in the best interest of all involved.

In his letter to the Colossians, Paul provided "rules of order" to help the family run smoothly. Paul believed that men and women, slave or free, were all one in Christ. He wrote to the Galatians, "There is neither Jew nor Greek, slave nor free, male nor female for you are all one in Christ Jesus."[1] This was a bold statement for the culture back then, which gave very little social status to slaves and women, and fiercely divided itself between Greeks and Jews. Yet Paul elevated those who were normally the underdogs, proclaiming a new freedom in Christ. Some Bible commentators believe that because of this newfound freedom, there was also newfound chaos and misuse of power. Order needed to be established, so Paul provided several guidelines. First concerning the family:

Colossians 3:18-21

Wives, submit to your husbands, as is fitting in the Lord. Husbands, love your wives and do not be harsh with them. Children, obey your parents in everything, for this pleases the Lord. Fathers, do not embitter your children, or they will become discouraged.

Paul laid out a system of leadership for a harmonious home, which exhibits the beauty and strength of order. He is not promoting a rigid or tyrannical system here, but rather one which encourages a mutual responsibility and love between the family members. In his book *Paul for Everyone,* author N.T. Wright talks about these guidelines:

What Paul is offering in this passage is a very brief Highway Code for household relationships. It is remarkable for several reasons. Perhaps the first is that he doesn't just tell wives, children and slaves how to behave (as many pagan moralists of his day would have done). Their duties are balanced by the corresponding duties of husbands, parents and masters.[2]

Some women reading this may balk at the very idea of the word "submit," seeing it as indicating some sort of subservience, but that's not what the word means at all. It literally translates "to subject oneself" and implies willingly putting yourself under someone or something. As a military term it means "to arrange in a military fashion under the command of a leader." Personally, I love the provision God has given us to willingly stand under the leadership of our husbands. God has lovingly given us a covering, a leader who must answer to God Himself. Equally, God gives the husband the mutual responsibility to love his wife and not be harsh with her.

There are several different types of love described in the Bible, but the love the husband is to have for his wife is *agape* love. It is the highest form of love, a selfless love, as in the sacrificial love Christ has for His church. A husband is not to lead like a dictator, lording it over his wife. Obviously if the husband loves his wife with a selfless *agape* love, the wife will willingly place herself under his authority. John Phillips writes this, "The sensible man will listen to his wife, respect her views, and consider her best interests when making decisions regarding the home. God holds him responsible, however, to exercise his headship, and the woman is responsible to submit to it."[3] Paul adds that husbands should not be harsh toward their wives, especially as leaders of the home. "Do not be harsh" actually means "do not be bitter or angrily resentful." A root of bitterness can destroy a family, so Paul instructed them to let go of bitterness.

Keep in mind that Paul is addressing husbands and wives in a family. He is not telling women to submit to all men or even other Christian men. These guidelines come to us in context of the family. He is not saying that women are subservient to men or considered inferior to men. He is simply giving guiding principles of order in the home. Submission certainly doesn't mean you cannot share your opinion. In fact, it is important for us as couples to support each other by respectfully sharing our opinions with one another in a nonargumentative way. We should see our role as building up one another.

Valid Questions

We can creatively think of all sorts of questions and exceptions concerning the area of submission.

- Should I submit to my husband if he doesn't show an *agape* type of love toward me?
- What if he is abusive?
- What if he wants me to do something illegal or immoral?
- What if he is not abusive but is a control freak?
- What if he is an idiot?
- What if he is not a Christian?

First let's address the question of the husband not doing his part. Then we will look at some of the exceptions. Paul did not write these guidelines as an "if-then" clause. He didn't say, "Husbands, love your wives only if they submit to your leadership." He told each member of the household what they were supposed to do while he also encouraged the balance of respect. Ultimately, every Christian, man or woman, child or parent, slave or free, is to submit to Christ's authority. He told the Ephesians to submit to one another out of reverence for Christ. When a wife respects her husband's leadership, more often than not he will respond in love. Equally, if husbands selflessly and lovingly lead in the home, their wives are much more likely to respect them. It's a beautiful balance that works. Bottom line, we should do our part even if we don't feel our husband is living up to his. But read on.

Let's take a look at some situations that may pose a problem in the area concerning the topic of submission. Keep in mind that just because there are exceptions to a rule, it doesn't mean the rule itself is faulty. People are faulty. We live in a world full of sin. Perfection will come in heaven, but here we must deal with old habits and sinful patterns that affect our relationships. There are several exceptions we must consider. For instance, if your husband is physically abusing you, then do not submit to his abuse. Get out and get help. There are also forms of psychological, emotional, or even spiritual abuse that I must note as well. Please seek biblical counseling or godly advice if you suspect you are living in this type of abusive situation.[4] (I recommend two of Leslie Vernick's books, *The Emotionally Destructive Relationship: Seeing It, Stopping It, Surviving It* and *How to Act Right When Your Husband Acts Wrong*.)

If your husband is asking you to do something illegal (cheat on tax returns, steal from a company, hold up a bank, etc.) or immoral (open marriage, adultery, pornography, child abuse, etc.) then you do not submit to him. Remember your ultimate authority is God Himself. If your husband is asking you to do something against God's authority, then you must obey God and not man.

"What if my husband is not a Christian—then do I have to be subject to his leadership?" Let me answer that question with another passage from Scripture. This is from Peter, who learned to submit his big, burly, strong will to Christ. Read what he has to say about the topic of submission. He begins by talking to both men and women:

1 PETER 2:13-17, 21-25

Submit yourselves for the Lord's sake to every authority instituted among men: whether to the king, as the supreme authority, or to governors, who are sent by him to punish those who do wrong and to commend those who do right. For it is God's will that by doing good you should silence the ignorant talk of foolish men. Live as free men, but do not use your freedom as a cover-up for evil; live as servants of God. Show proper respect to everyone: Love the brotherhood of believers, fear God, honor the king...

To this you were called, because Christ suffered for you, leaving you an example, that you should follow in his steps. "He committed no sin, and no deceit was found in his mouth." When they hurled their insults at him, he did not retaliate; when he suffered, he made no threats. Instead, he entrusted himself to him who judges justly. He himself bore our sins in his body on the tree, so that we might die to sins and live for righteousness; by his wounds you have been healed. For you were like sheep going astray, but now you have returned to the Shepherd and Overseer of your souls.

Notice that Peter uses the example of Christ as a picture of the beauty of submission. Now let's see what Peter specifically says to wives, especially wives with unbelieving husbands.

1 PETER 3:1-6

Wives, in the same way be submissive to your husbands so that, if any of them do not believe the word, they may be won over without words by the behavior of their wives, when they see the purity and reverence of your lives. Your beauty should not come from outward adornment, such as braided hair and the wearing of gold jewelry and fine clothes. Instead, it should be that of your inner self, the unfading beauty of a gentle and quiet spirit, which is of great worth in God's sight. For this is the way the holy women of the past who put their hope in God used to make themselves beautiful. They were submissive to their own husbands, like Sarah, who obeyed Abraham and called him her master. You are her daughters if you do what is right and do not give way to fear.

Many a man has been drawn to Christ through the loving, gentle, and submissive attitude of his wife. One other piece of advice I want us to notice from Peter. Did you catch his beauty tip for us? He said that lasting beauty does not come from outward external stuff like makeup, hair, clothes, and the perfect body; it comes from a different source. Confident and unfading beauty comes from a gentle and quiet spirit, which is of great worth in God's sight. Women in the Old Testament who hoped in God had this kind of beauty. We too can experience a beyond-the-surface beauty as we put our hope in God. Our hope in God is evidenced in a gentle and quiet spirit. Not a doormat! Not a defiant woman, but a woman of strength and dignity who finds her confidence in the Lord. It takes great strength to be gentle and quiet in the way we approach others, but if the peace of God is refereeing our heart we are able to walk in confidence.

Children, Obedience, and Encouragement

Parenting is no easy job. It takes wisdom, patience, and responsibility on the part of the parents with the end goal to raise children who honor God with their lives. Once again, Paul is providing principles for order in the home. How many of us have seen those families where the children seem to rule the roost? What the kids want, they get. Respecting others and obeying rules has been replaced with blaming others and lack of responsibility. In their book entitled *It's Not My Fault*, Drs. Henry Cloud and John Townsend share the importance of teaching children to take ownership of their actions.

> What seems like just a common, no-harm-done excuse— "It's not my fault!"—is often a dangerous trap because people don't recognize what the blaming mindset does to them. It not only keeps them from overcoming the effects of all that they can't control—like other people, circumstances and genetics—but separates them from a solution. And when they give away the ownership of their life, they end up losing the one opportunity they have to fulfill their dreams and enjoy God's best.[5]

Obedience—it's a beautiful thing. We must teach our kids when they are young to take ownership of their actions. We must deliberately and lovingly teach them to obey God, to obey authority, and to obey the rules of the house. Even Jesus subjected Himself to His parents' authority. You may remember the story found in the book of Luke. Jesus at 12 years old was in Jerusalem for the Passover with his parents, but when it was time for everyone to go home He stayed behind, visiting with the Jewish leaders. His parents didn't realize He was missing because they assumed He was probably with other family members. When they finally found Him in the temple, He asked them, "Didn't you know I had to be in My Father's house?" The Scripture goes on to say, "Then he went down to Nazareth with them and was obedient to them. But his mother treasured all these things in her heart. And Jesus grew in wisdom and stature, and in favor with God and men."[6]

Jesus, the Son of God, was obedient to His parents. Isn't that amazing to think about? Once again Christ gives us an example to follow. Notice He grew in wisdom and in favor with both God and people. I have to wonder if those qualities grew from a heart of obedience. Obedience to God and wisdom go hand in hand, since the fear of the Lord is the beginning of wisdom. We must wisely seek God's direction in raising our kids to obey the house rules, and more importantly, to obey God's rules.

As Paul gives balance to each guideline here in Colossians, we also see the responsibility of the parents. The fathers are addressed here, but we mothers too can heed this warning. Steer clear of exasperating our kids or embittering them with ridiculous rules and regulations. Personally I see many parents who set rules and parent out of fear. In his book *Grace-Based Parenting,* Tim Kimmel says, "Christians frequently believe that the battle for a child's heart and soul is fought on the outside—with rigid rules and boundaries—when in fact just the opposite is true."[7] He encourages families to communicate the unconditional love that Christ offers and affirm God's grace in the home.

Many times kids rebel because their hearts have become bitter and discouraged through over-the-top discipline and rules. They don't feel loved, they feel dominated. They don't feel that their parents see them for who they really are and what they can do. They feel like their parents only see what they *can't* do. When I think about how God deals with us, He looks at our hearts, and He disciplines in love. Discipline and wise rules show that we love our kids; unnecessary rules show that we are afraid. Three books have really made sense to me in the area of discipline and why kids rebel: Tim Kimmel's *Grace-Based Parenting* and *Why Christian Kids Rebel,* and Tedd Tripp's *Shepherding Your Child's Heart.*

The flip side of discouraging your child is to encourage them, giving them strength through your words and your support to be who God created them to be. Solomon said, "Train a child in the way he should go, and when he is old he will not turn from it."[8] In a broader sense, there are only two ways to go, the way of wisdom and obedience or the way of a fool and evil inclinations. We must train our children to go down the path of wisdom, obedience, and righteousness. The expression "way he should go" can be rendered as "according to his way." In this case we can understand the importance of recognizing the gifts, talents, and abilities of each of our children and encouraging them in that direction.

It is our job as parents to be encouragers rather than discouragers. Encouraging obedience, wisdom, righteousness, along with their gifts, talents, and abilities. Loving and wise discipline along with godly leadership will bring great encouragement to our children's hearts. We must not discourage and embitter our children through harsh or cruel discipline or even unreasonable rules. Prayerfully seek God's wisdom day by day as you parent your children. (I invite you to visit my website created especially for moms, www.PositiveMom.com, for more helpful parenting tips and ideas.)

The Joy of Work

W. Clement Stone said, "There is very little difference in people. But that little difference makes a big difference. The little difference is attitude. The big difference is whether it is positive or negative."[9] What is your attitude toward work? Often we think of work in the context of drudgery and difficulty, but Paul encouraged Christians to look at work with a different attitude. He said, "Whatever you do, work at it with all your heart, as working for the Lord, not for men." When we look at our work from that perspective, our attitude becomes more positive.

As you read this next passage, please understand that Paul is not condoning slavery. We need to understand the context of the times. Sadly, the majority of the workforce throughout the entire Roman Empire was made up of people who had no rights of their own, but were considered property or slaves. At this point Paul didn't deal with the social concern of slavery. Rather, he is giving spiritual direction and practical guidelines for both masters and slaves in the context of the culture. Keep in mind Paul considered Christian freemen and slaves as one in Christ. Faith in Christ transcends all strata of society.

The message translates for us today into the obligations of employee and employer. Here's Paul's word to both:

COLOSSIANS 3:22–4:1

Slaves, obey your earthly masters in everything; and do it, not only when their eye is on you and to win their favor, but with sincerity of heart and reverence for the Lord. Whatever you do, work at it with all your heart, as working for the Lord, not for men, since you know that you will receive an inheritance from the Lord as a reward. It is the Lord Christ you are serving. Anyone who does wrong will be repaid for his wrong, and there is no favoritism. Masters, provide your slaves with what is right and fair, because you know that you also have a Master in heaven.

Will Rogers said, "In order to succeed, you must know what you are doing, like what you are doing, and believe in what you are doing."[10] We can believe in what we are doing and like what we are doing when we recognize who our true employer is. When we are working for God it changes things. First, we know that God is the One who sees all. We know that ultimately our reward will come from Him. If we are working simply to get a paycheck, we will grow weary. If we are working to get ahead and impress the boss, we are performing, and we may also be guilty of pushing down others. But when we work for the Lord, we work with excellence because He is excellent and because we love Him. We work in His strength, seeking His guidance and wisdom all along the way.

Christians ought to be the best employees, giving their very best as well as working with a great attitude. Television show host Art Linkletter had a great philosophy when it comes to work. He said,

> Do a little more than you're paid to;
> Give a little more than you have to;
> Try a little harder than you want to;
> Aim a little higher than you think possible;
> And give a lot of thanks to God for health,
>   family and friends.[11]

Sounds like he listened to Paul's words to the Colossians, doesn't it? There is great joy and satisfaction in meaningful, hard work. Don't detest your work—look instead at how you can serve God through your work. I'm reminded of Brother Lawrence, who worked as one of the kitchen help in a monastery in seventeenth-century France. He saw all of his work as an opportunity to experience God's presence and to praise and glorify Him. Even in the mundane work of the kitchen he found great joy. (You can still read his writings today in a book called *Practicing the Presence of God.*)

Paul reminds everyone that those who do wrong will be repaid for their wrong and that there is no favoritism with God. I believe this is a reminder to both the employee and employer. We serve the Lord Christ, and He is the God who sees all things. We may try to hide our actions from people, but God sees everything—you can't hide from Him. This not only keeps us honest, but also reassures us that we can trust our sovereign God if we have been treated unfairly. He doesn't show favoritism because of social status or race. We can trust Him to repay the wrongs done to us.

Of course, Paul always gives the balancing responsibility, so he speaks to employers' obligation as well. Christian bosses must recognize that they answer to God. They are to provide what is fair and right to their employees. This can cover compensation as well as safety and good work conditions. Think about how well a company would run if both the employees and employer heeded Paul's guidelines. We probably wouldn't have all the labor issues that plague our workplaces today. Consider Sophie's story as a cheerful reminder of who we serve.

Sophie's True Boss

Sophie the "scrubwoman," as she was called, faithfully scrubbed the steps of the large New York City building on her hands and knees every day. One day a fellow Christian passed by and said to her, "Sophie, I understand that you are a child of God."

"Yes, sir, I'm a child of the King!" she responded with enthusiasm.

The man replied, "Well since you are a child of the King, don't you believe that God recognizes you as a princess?"

"He certainly does!" beamed Sophie.

"Well, if God is your Father, and you are a princess and a child of the King, don't you think that it is beneath your level to be found here in New York City scrubbing these dirty steps?"

None daunted, Sophie replied, "There's no humiliation whatever. You see, I'm not scrubbing these steps for Mr. Brown, my boss. I'm scrubbing them for Jesus Christ, my Savior!"[12]

Looks like Sophie was familiar with Colossians as well! There is great joy in service when we see it as serving our King, the one who loves us and gave His life for us. Serve with confidence in the place God has sent you, with the gifts He has given you, in the strength He provides for you.

Confident Steps

ADDITIONAL READING: Ephesians 5—Positive guidelines for harmonious homes

BATTLE FOR THE TRUTH:

Confidence Defeater—*I shouldn't have to answer to anyone. I can live as I please.*

Confidence Builder—Confidence is strengthened when we lovingly and wisely relate to the people closest to us and willingly subject ourselves to Christ.

CHOICES:

- Submit to God's authority.
- Willingly be subject to those God has placed in authority over you.
- Seek counseling and get help if you are in a difficult or abusive situation.
- Parent with love and grace, encouraging obedience and righteousness.
- Work heartily as for the Lord and not for man.

- Remember that God sees all—He will repay.
- Provide what is right and fair for those who work for you.
- Joyfully serve the Lord and others.

DELIBERATE PLAN: Self-survey on submission.

Take some time to carefully look at both your family relationships and your work relationships. Are there any areas you need to prayerfully submit to the Lord's leadership? Are there any of these guidelines you have been ignoring or you need to face? Ask the Lord to give you the will and the grace to live as He has called you to live.

$\mathcal{M}$astering Meaningful Conversations with God and Man

"The words of a man's mouth are deep waters,
But the fountain of wisdom is a bubbling brook."

Proverbs 18:4

"There may be no single thing more important
in our efforts to achieve meaningful work
and fulfilling relationships than to learn
to practice the art of communication."

Max DePree

Have you ever fumbled for the right words to say in an awkward situation? Or maybe I should rephrase the question—*When is the last time* you fumbled for the right words to say in an awkward situation? I'm talking about times like this: You ask a woman when the baby is due as you pat her stomach, and she replies, "I'm not pregnant." Or you're standing next to someone at an art gallery and comment, "This isn't art; even I could do this"—and he introduces himself as the artist.

Sometimes it's best just to keep your mouth closed, rather than putting both feet there. I like what Dorothy Nevill had to say, "The real art of conversation is not only to say the right thing in the right place, but to leave unsaid the wrong thing at the tempting moment." I wish I were better at that!

Words are powerful. Choose them wisely. The apostle James wrote about the power of the tongue using all sorts of analogies. Here's what he said:

> *When we put bits into the mouths of horses to make them obey us, we can turn the whole animal. Or take ships as an example. Although they are so large and are driven by strong winds, they are steered by a very small rudder wherever the pilot wants to go. Likewise the tongue is a small part of the body, but it makes great boasts. Consider what a great forest is set on fire by a small spark. The tongue also is a fire, a world of evil among the parts of the body. It corrupts the whole person, sets the whole course of his life on fire, and is itself set on fire by hell.*
>
> *All kinds of animals, birds, reptiles and creatures of the sea are being tamed and have been tamed by man, but no man can tame the tongue.* [1]

Thankfully, with God's help we can use our words to build up rather than tear down. We can bring strength, hope, and comfort to others. As we talked about earlier, our words are an overflow of what is in our heart, so when we allow God to change and purify our hearts, our words grow ever more sweet. Part of that purifying process happens as we spend time alone with God, enjoying His presence and drawing near to Him. Our conversations with God through prayer begin to change us into more gracious, purposeful, and confident women, and as a result our conversations with people are more meaningful and uplifting.

The Most Important Conversation

The first conversation of the day is the most important one, and by that I mean the conversation of prayer. Talking with God sets the tone for the rest of your day. Prayer ought to be such an important part of our day that we feel starved without it. It is our daily strength and nourishment for our soul. Sixteenth-century contemplative writer Teresa of Avila said, "Souls without prayer are like people whose bodies or limbs are paralyzed: they possess feet and hands but they cannot control them."

It seems that for many Christians, prayer is set aside as inconvenient or as an inefficient use of time. A 2010 Gallup poll reveals that 83 percent of Americans believe there is a God who answers prayer.[2] I wonder how many of those people actually do pray. Oh yes, I think we all believe in prayer when we are facing a disaster or a challenge of some sort. That's a good time to pray for sure! But day in, day out, the hard work of prayer isn't on the schedule for many people. Could it be that because prayer is done in the secret places there is little motivation to participate? We get no accolades from the world for private time alone with God. We don't get paid for it, and no one sees that we have accomplished it. We don't get stars by our name or applause from an audience.

Paul believed in the importance and the power of prayer. Not only was he a prayer warrior himself, but he also urged Christians to earnestly pray and seek God:

Colossians 4:2-4

Devote yourselves to prayer, being watchful and thankful. And pray for us, too, that God may open a door for our message, so that we may proclaim the mystery of Christ, for which I am in chains. Pray that I may proclaim it clearly, as I should.

Janet Evans got up at 4:45 a.m. six days a week in order to swim 6000 meters before school, and then returned to the pool after classes for another rigorous workout. Her devotion paid off, as she won three gold medals in the 1988 Olympics. By the end of her career, she held seven world records, five Olympic medals (including four gold), and forty-five U.S. national titles. Janet's passion for swimming started when she was three years old, but it was her devotion to it that led to her accomplishments. It's one thing to be excited about a sport; it's another thing to be devoted to it.

Devotion requires commitment, action, and discipline. For an athlete it may mean getting up early for morning workouts, and then working out again later in the day. It means working out even when you don't feel like it. It means doing the stuff behind the scenes that no one else sees. Rare is the athlete who can simply jump in the game and perform at the finest level without devotion to practice. Rare is the Christian who can carry on the work of Christ without a devotion to prayer. Writer and preacher J.C. Ryle said, "Never, never may we forget that if we would do good to the world, our first duty is to pray."[3]

As a business leader, my dad often says, "It takes a lot of unspectacular preparation to see spectacular results." Athletes must diligently work out in their practices, so that when they are on the field or in competition they have the strength and agility to perform well. In a similar way, when a Christian woman is devoted to prayer, we begin to see the spectacular results in the form of wisdom, faith, and a peace that passes all understanding. A woman who is devoted to prayer rarely gets shaken by unplanned disappointments, nor does she fall apart when she gets unexpected bad news. A woman of prayer has an anchor deep within her soul, a confidence only God can give.

Paul told the Colossians to devote themselves to prayer. In other words, to throw themselves wholeheartedly into prayer. "Devote" is the Greek word *proskartereo*, which means to be courageously persistent or to hold fast and not let go. Picture a bulldog holding on to his favorite bone. He's not going to let go! Perhaps an even better analogy would be the way I hold on to my cell phone. I wouldn't go anywhere without it, would you? Perhaps we should earnestly hold on to prayer in that same manner. E.M. Bounds was known as a man of prayer, and he often prayed for several hours early in the morning before he began his work. He said, "To pray is the greatest thing we can do, and to do it well, there must be calmness, time, and deliberation." Calmness and time seem to be two rare commodities in today's hurry-up, gotta-go culture. Let us be devoted to being still and knowing that He is God.

Devotion to prayer also refers to persistence in prayer. That doesn't mean wearing God down by asking, asking, asking until you get what you want. What it does mean is continually bringing our needs to the Lord. Don't give up. Jesus said,

> *Keep on asking, and you will receive what you ask for. Keep on seeking, and you will find. Keep on knocking, and the door will be opened to you. For everyone who asks, receives. Everyone who seeks, finds. And to everyone who knocks, the door will be opened.*
>
> *You parents—if your children ask for a loaf of bread, do you give them a stone instead? Or if they ask for a fish, do you give them a snake? Of course not! So if you sinful people know how to give good gifts to your children, how much more will your heavenly Father give good gifts to those who ask him.*[4]

What a generous invitation! The God of all creation has given us an invitation to converse with Him, to share our thankfulness and our burdens. Let us not ignore such a glorious invitation to meet with Him each day in fellowship and communion. David declared, "How priceless is your unfailing love! Both high and low among men find refuge in the shadow of your wings. They feast on the abundance of your house; you give them drink from your river of delights. For with you is the fountain of life; in your light we see light."[5] Isn't it marvelous to think He invites us to His table, to feast from the abundance of His house and drink from His river of delights? Oh, how little we ask, how little we receive!

Be Watchful

Why is it so hard to get to sleep when I have something important to do early the next day, but so easy to fall asleep when I'm praying? Can you relate? Don't feel too bad—the disciples had the same problem. Jesus took them to the Garden of Gethsemane as He prepared for the cross, and He asked them to pray while He went a distance away to pray alone. "My soul is overwhelmed with sorrow to the point of death," He said to them. "Stay here and keep watch." But when He returned to His disciples and found them sleeping He said, "Could you not keep watch for one hour? Watch and pray so that you will not fall into temptation. The spirit is willing, but the body is weak."[6]

What good words for us to heed today—"Watch and pray so that you will not fall into temptation." Meditating on God's Word and praying are two ways that help us be aware of temptation. Paul told the Colossians to be watchful or vigilant in prayer. The words generally mean to stay awake while praying, implying to stay alert and focused. Prayer helps us stay alert to the schemes of the enemy, like a watchman in a tower. What is the best way to stay focused during your prayer time? For me, sometimes I like to pray while I am walking. It is a good way to stay focused and awake. I also like to get on my knees and pray, which is another position that keeps me focused. I'm definitely more alert in the morning, so that's my best prayer time, especially before anyone else is awake. Find the time, place, and position that work best for you.

Staying alert and watchful can also refer to being aware of the needs around you and praying about them. Be on the lookout for opportunities to pray for or with someone. Paul told the church at Thessalonica to pray without ceasing. Don't stop praying throughout your day. When you have coffee with a friend and she tells you that her marriage is in shambles, pray with her. When you talk with a family member who is trying to figure out their next career move, offer to pray with him. When you get an e-mail about an acquaintance who has just been diagnosed with cancer, stop and pray for her. When you are driving in the car alone and you begin to worry about your children, pray for them while you are driving (only don't close your eyes!). When you see someone who seems discouraged or lonely, offer a prayer to God for them in your heart. Pray, pray throughout your day.

When you see an accident happen in front of you, you never forget it. Several years ago when we were in Austin, Texas, we were driving to a friend's wedding when all of the sudden we heard a big boom and saw a car spinning out of control. The next thing we knew, there was a body lying facedown on the pavement. Curt and I were some of the first people on the scene to help. We called 9-1-1, and as Curt checked the other cars, I went over to the woman on the pavement. She was breathing heavily, and I knew that she might have neck or back injuries so I didn't try to move her. We found her name from the belongings that had flown from her car, so I began comforting her with my words and praying for her by name. Others began gathering to see if they could help, and in the gravity of the situation they just bowed their heads and listened to my prayer.

The paramedics arrived quickly and we stepped aside. Although we couldn't do anymore to help, we knew we could pray, and that we did. We were not able to find out what happened to her, but the God who sees all knows how everything turned out. Although we may feel helpless in some ways, we are never helpless when we can pray. Curt and I continued to pray for her and her family for a while after the accident. There is comfort in knowing we can confidently talk to our heavenly Father on anyone's behalf. Be on the alert. Watch and pray.

And Be Thankful

Do you think Paul is trying to make a point here? How many times does he remind the Colossians to be thankful? I counted seven in this short book. Why in the world does he think being thankful is so important? Perhaps he recognizes that being thankful can literally change the way we view life. Being thankful can have an effect on our relationships with both God and man. Think about it—a grateful person is a joy to be around. She is confident, happy, and hopeful. An ungrateful person is miserable to be around because she typically whines and complains.

Being a thankful person means that you thank God not only for the good stuff—although most people forget to do that—but it also means being thankful in the middle of the more challenging situations. Paul gave thanks as a prisoner. He told the people in Thessalonica to give thanks in all circumstances, for this was God's will for them in Christ Jesus. He told the Philippians to pray and give thanks in the midst of their worries.

God loves a grateful heart. The psalmist wrote,

> *Make thankfulness your sacrifice to God,*
> *and keep the vows you made to the Most High.*
> *Then call on me when you are in trouble,*
> *and I will rescue you,*
> *and you will give me glory...*

But giving thanks is a sacrifice that truly honors me.
If you keep to my path,
I will reveal to you the salvation of God. [7]

Jesus made a startling comment that always comes to mind when I think about being a grateful person. In Luke we read His words as He described God's kindness to all people, saying, "He is kind to the ungrateful and the wicked."[8] Notice how He lumped together the ungrateful and the wicked. Ouch—I wouldn't want to be in that category. And remember what Jesus said about the ten lepers who were healed when only one, a Samaritan, returned to say thank-you. "Jesus asked, 'Were not all ten cleansed? Where are the other nine? Was no one found to return and give praise to God except this foreigner?' Then he said to him, 'Rise and go; your faith has made you well.'"[9] Interestingly, it was the despised Samaritan who returned and fell at Jesus' feet to say thank-you. God is pleased with our thankfulness, not our status.

Yes, gratitude is big in God's eyes. Think about it—don't you love it when someone recognizes you have done something kind for them? It shows they noticed. God is continually doing kind things for us. We can begin each day by thanking Him for the new day, and for forgiveness of our sins, and for a fresh start, and for His merciful, gracious love for us, and for the way He has provided for our needs over the last 24 hours, and for the fact that He is continually with us, and that He has given us a mind to think with and gifts to use and hearts to know Him. Whew—that's just for starters! We have so much to thank Him for, we could be thanking Him every moment of every day.

Pray for Me

How often do you have people ask you to pray for them? I hope that happens often, because that would mean they are aware that you do pray. Paul asked the Colossians to pray for him. He had a good mutual praying relationship with them. As you remember, he started off his letter telling them how he prays for them. And what a powerful prayer it was! At the end of his letter he asked them to exchange the favor. How would you like to be prayer partners with Paul?

Do you have a prayer partner? I want to encourage you to ask one or two of your praying friends to be a prayer partner. I have several dear friends I can call or e-mail and say, "I need prayer as I speak here or teach there." I can't tell you what a blessing it is to have their encouragement and prayer support. And I pray for them as well. We all need it. Paul needed it, Jesus needed it, and we do too.

My friend Sharon Hill is most definitely a prayer warrior. She has started a ministry called OnCall Prayer.™ She developed the name after a time of much prayer (no surprise), when a great idea came to her. She thought about how often we call a business and are put on hold or have to leave a message—but God is always on call. He is always available to hear our prayers anytime, anyplace. She not only developed an efficient and unique prayer journal, but she also came up with the concept of forming a prayer shield for those who serve in Christian ministry. Here's how she describes it:

> As a Christian leader on the front lines of ministry, you are more vulnerable to spiritual warfare. Those in ministry are more accountable, have more responsibility, are often subject to greater temptation, often suffer fatigue and/or burnout, and are often criticized. Specifically requesting prayer from a Prayer Shield—a designated team of three intercessors—provides a prayer covering, creates strength, and ensures victorious living. "Though one may be overpowered, two can defend themselves. A cord of three strands is not easily broken." Ecclesiastes 4:12.[10]

When we pray for our friends we begin to develop a deeper bond with them. Friendships are enhanced and strengthened as we are open and honest with one another about our needs. Paul, the big-time apostle, made himself vulnerable by asking for prayer. It takes humility to ask for someone to pray for you because it shows that you know you have needs and are looking to God for help. Praying for one another builds a bond of love between you. That's why I encourage married couples to pray together every night before they go to bed. Prayer also gives you the opportunity to rejoice together as you watch God at work.

A recent study confirms this by documenting that in fact the old adage is true, couples who pray together actually do tend to stay together.[11]

Paul's prayer request was genuine, not selfish or self-centered. He asked the Colossians to pray for opportunities to share the mystery of Christ. He also asked them to pray that he proclaim the gospel clearly. Paul, Mr. Eloquent Speaker himself, was asking for prayer that he proclaim it clearly? After reading all of his letters, I'm not worried about his ability to communicate the gospel, are you? But he recognized he wasn't perfect and he needed God's help to proclaim the truth. He sincerely wanted to spread the gospel with clarity so many would understand and know Christ. We need that same prayer, don't we?

> *Father, give us the ability to share the*
> *truth about Jesus, clearly and wisely.*

Make the Most of Every Opportunity

What do unbelievers think about Christians? Sadly, Christians are often viewed as hateful, judgmental, self-serving people by those who do not know Christ. Christians have become known for what they are against, instead of what they are for. Needless to say most people don't think of them as people who love Jesus and want to demonstrate His love to the world. In fact, this week in the news, a bestselling secular novelist declared publicly that she is distancing herself from Christianity because she doesn't agree with Christians' judgmental attitudes. She said she still believes in Christ and reads the Bible; she just doesn't want to be associated with religion and Christianity.

Looks like we have an image problem. Now to be sure, there is a delicate balance between standing on the principles of God's Word and lovingly relating to those who do not adhere to the Bible. True followers of Christ ought to be seen as people who reflect Christ's image—gracious, loving, humble, and kind. We need to live righteous lives and honor Him with our obedience. Notice I did not say self-righteous or holier-than-thou lives. Our words and actions must show the world what Jesus looked like. People would be hungry for Christ if they saw believers who reflected Him in both grace and truth.

Paul was as concerned about how Christians reflected Christ back in his day as we should be concerned about our reflection today. Here's what he wrote:

COLOSSIANS 4:5-6

Be wise in the way you act toward outsiders; make the most of every opportunity. Let your conversation be always full of grace, seasoned with salt, so that you may know how to answer everyone.

"Walk wisely" is what Paul was actually saying. How do we walk wisely? By walking with Christ and living in obedience to Him, and not spewing out hateful judgments toward others. The world needs to see a picture of what righteousness looks like, rather than hearing us talk about it. Unfortunately, Christians look like the rest of the world in many ways.

Paul tells us to walk in a manner worthy of our calling. Our job is not to demand Christian values of outsiders as much as it is to demand them of ourselves personally. What if the world saw Christian marriages staying together or Christians living with integrity at work or Christians loving their neighbors as themselves? One area I do see Christians being a good example is in the area of reaching out to help those in need. Christian service has made a significant difference in our nation and in the world. May we continue to bless the world with Christ's compassion and bless them with our words as well.

Our conversation must be gracious toward outsiders. When we talk to people who do not know Christ (well, actually, when we talk to *anyone*) our words and tone must be filled with grace. Grace doesn't simply mean being nice, it means showing unmerited favor, the kind of grace God has for us. When I think of grace I think of speaking with mercy and forgiveness to others and embracing them where they are at in their lives. Accepting them as people and compassionately caring for them. Caring for their heart and not just thinking of them as "someone who needs to get their act together" or "someone I can win over to Christianity."

Our conversation is also to be seasoned with salt. I love, love, love popcorn, but popcorn without salt in my opinion is not worth eating. It's just bland and tasteless. Salt brings out the flavor in foods, just like wise words bring flavor and enrichment to a conversation. I love to talk (almost as much as I love popcorn), but I don't enjoy meaningless conversations. A conversation seasoned with salt has substance and purpose. I believe the best conversations happen when we are focused on the interests of the other person. Ask them questions about themselves, draw them out, and find out what makes them tick. They will be drawn to you, and you will begin to understand their needs. Look for opportunities to sprinkle blessings of truth throughout the conversation.

Several years ago I was speaking in Florida. But I was also in the midst of writing a book, so on the plane trip home I had my Bible on my lap, ready to study and write. I do realize that plane trips offer wonderful opportunities to open up conversation about the Lord, not in a pushy way at all, but in the natural course of conversation. I think I could write an entire book about the amazing things God has done through conversations on planes during my travels. On this particular flight a man sat down next to me and immediately wanted to talk. He saw my Bible, which gave him the first topic of conversation.

He began asking me what I believed, and I told him. I in turn asked him about his beliefs. It became evident quite quickly that he respected the Bible, but he was not a Christian. He came from a Jewish background but had left most of that for a mixture of his own philosophies and religions blended together. It's kind of like he went to a salad bar displaying all the religions of the world and simply took the items he wanted from each. We talked about heaven and hell and what Jesus had to say, but then at a certain point we began talking about why Jesus came to this earth. Was He just a good man, or was He the Son of God? And why did He die on the cross?

God was in charge of this whole plane trip, and I believe He wanted us to have more time to talk, so when we were told that our plane couldn't land in Dallas because of a storm I wasn't surprised. The plane was diverted to Austin to get more fuel and then eventually back to Dallas. The three-hour ride turned into about a five-hour journey. The cool thing was that they did show a movie on the flight in order to keep everyone happy. Of all things, the movie was *The Lion, the Witch and the Wardrobe*, part of the Chronicles of Narnia by C.S. Lewis. If you know the story, Aslan the lion is a type of Christ figure, and at a certain point he willingly offers his life as a sacrifice to save the people of Narnia.

Only God could have orchestrated the timing on this. Just as I was in deep conversation with this man about why Christ sacrificed his life for us, I looked up on the screen, and there was Aslan giving his life on behalf of the people. I said, "Look," pointed to the screen, and related the whole picture of Christ and His love for us. What a perfect opportunity! Thank You, Lord. God was at work in that man's life, and He allowed me to play a part in planting seeds of the gospel message. No, the man did not trust Christ right then and there, but I am sure God continued to lead him to the truth of the gospel.

Make the most of every opportunity through the words God gives you. Be alert, be aware, be wise. We prepare through prayer, for it is God who gives us the eyes to see the opportunities and gives us wisdom to share His truth. It is God who gives us a gracious spirit, for He is full of grace. It is God who waters the seed and brings the harvest. We may not be the one who gets to see a person come to faith in Christ, but we can have the joy of planting seeds and seasoning the conversation with salt. At the end of the long flight from Florida, as we were waiting for our bags, the man gave me a hug and said he knew we were supposed to meet. It is always a joy to be used by God, when we make the most of every opportunity.

Confident Steps

ADDITIONAL READING: Matthew 7—Jesus teaches about prayer and people

BATTLE FOR THE MIND:

Confidence Defeater—*I don't have time to pray. I can get along fine without it.*

Confidence Builder—Our confidence in conversations with people is strengthened through our private conversations with God.

CHOICES:

- Be devoted to prayer like an athlete is devoted to preparation.
- Be watchful and focused.
- Develop a deliberate attitude of gratitude.
- Build a prayer team of support.
- Be wise in the way you act toward outsiders.
- Make the most of every opportunity.
- Create meaningful conversations.

DELIBERATE PLAN: Thankfulness journal.

Take deliberate steps to being a more thankful person. Begin each day by writing down at least five things that you are thankful for in your life. Make it a daily practice as a part of your daily prayer routine. Set aside a time and a place for thankfulness and prayer each day.

Part Six

Shine with Joy

*"The thief comes only to steal and kill and destroy;
I have come so that they may have life,
and may have it abundantly."*

John 10:10 net

*"The joy that Jesus gives is the result of our disposition
being at one with his own disposition."*

Oswald Chambers

$\mathcal{R}$ecognize the Blessing You Bring to This World

*"Each of you should look not only to your own interests,
but also to the interests of others."*
PHILIPPIANS 2:4

*"Do not let what you cannot do interfere
with what you can do."*
JOHN WOODEN

You've heard of the Big Ten, the Top Ten, and the Perfect Ten—now we are going to take a look at the Parting Ten. Yes, you read that right. As Paul closes his letter to the Colossians he has some parting words concerning ten of his friends. Normally I skip over this kind of stuff. I mean, seriously, who really reads the credits at the end of a movie except maybe the mother of the set designer or the proud uncle of the key grip? Most people leave when the movie is over. Just because it is time for the credit lines, that doesn't mean the powerful truths in God's Word have diminished. Take it from me, one who always skims through Paul's credits, there are tremendous blessings here you don't want to miss. Even more importantly, there are some significant life applications we all can take personally.

Each of the people Paul addressed in his closing statements offers a life lesson that can make a difference in our own journey. Each one of the Parting Ten had specific talents and personalities that God used to make a difference in the lives of others, and we too have been equipped with unique gifts He can use to allow us to be a blessing to this world. In this chapter we are going to dig a little deeper than just looking at the names and salutations that Paul delivered. I'm going to pull together information from other scriptures in which the Parting Ten are mentioned. In this way we can get a bit of a sketch of their lives and learn how God used their gifts and how God can use us as well. These are going to be the most enriching credit lines you have ever read!

1. Tychicus—A Portrait of Loyalty and Faithfulness

Loyalty and faithfulness are rare qualities in today's world. From switching churches, changing jobs, or leaving spouses, in many ways we have replaced loyalty with "what's best for me." I know there are times when we do need to make a job change or look for a new congregation—and we need prayerful direction from God in those matters—but faithfulness is a strong and beautiful quality. Tychicus was a man of faith who was also faithful to the ministry and to God's people. Here's how Paul described him:

> Tychicus will tell you all the news about me. He is a dear brother, a faithful minister and fellow servant in the Lord. I am sending him to you for the express purpose that you may know about our circumstances and that he may encourage your hearts.[1]

As one of Paul's personal representatives, Tychicus most likely was the one chosen to deliver Paul's letters to both the Ephesians and the Colossians. He wasn't only delivering Paul's letters, he was also supposed to give a report about Paul. You have to really trust someone's loyalty if you are depending on them to bring information about you to others. How easy it is for someone to take a portion of the truth and twist it to make another look bad and make himself look good. Paul had full confidence in his friend Tychicus. In the book of Acts we also learn that Tychicus traveled with Paul to Jerusalem. Paul wrote to Timothy and Titus telling them he was sending Tychicus to them too. Boy, Tychicus was one busy guy! But that's because Paul could trust him as a faithful servant to carry out the tasks he gave him.

Tychicus was also sent to encourage the hearts of the Colossian believers. His job was to strengthen their hearts with God's truth. I have a feeling that God's truth dwelt richly in Tychicus life and that is why he was a faithful friend and encourager. Tychicus was the type of man who enriched other people's lives, bringing truth and encouragement. A trusted and faithful encourager is a blessing to the body of Christ, strengthening and building up rather than tearing down and dismantling. Let us be builders through our words and faithful actions.

Questions to ask yourself: Am I trustworthy? Do I use my words to build up, strengthen, and encourage others? Do I delight in good juicy stories, or do I delight in sharing God's truth? Who can I trust as a loyal friend? Paul had a friend he could rely on to tell the facts about his situation. We need to surround ourselves with trustworthy and faithful people. If your friend is telling stories to you about other people, then she is probably telling other people stories about you. I admit I try to distance myself from those whom I detect are not loyal friends. We must also examine ourselves and consider, Am I a loyal friend? Do I improperly share stories about others? Can I be trusted by my friends? Determine to guard your mouth and use it only to encourage others. Be loyal in your actions, beginning with your own family.

2. Onesimus—A Changed Life—Useless to Useful

Never underestimate the power of God to change a person's life. Onesimus was actually a hometown boy from Colossae, but he was also a runaway slave. He had run off from his owner, Philemon, a follower of Christ there. After meeting Paul in Rome, Onesimus became a believer in Christ and began wholeheartedly following Him. Paul sent him back to his owner and sent with him the letter to Philemon. He asked Philemon to receive back his former slave and forgive him for leaving. It is interesting to read that Paul identified Onesimus as a faithful and beloved brother and entrusted him also to share the information of what was happening in Rome. In a short period of time, Paul must have seen an evidence of a transformed life in Onesimus. Here are the words with which he included him as one of the Parting Ten:

> He [Tychicus] is coming with Onesimus, our faithful and dear brother, who is one of you. They will tell you everything that is happening here.[2]

A slave and now a fugitive, Onesimus was willing to do the right thing and return to his owner. The name *Onesimus* means "profitable." In his letter to Philemon, Paul wrote, "I appeal to you for my son Onesimus, who became my son while I was in chains. Formerly he was useless to you, but now he has become useful both to you and to me. I am sending him—who is my very heart—back to you."[3] Think about it— once he was useless to his owner, but now he has become useful. What made the difference? Christ! Through Christ, Onesimus had become a new creation and a very dear help to Paul. Once a rebellious spirit, now Onesimus had a faithful and serving heart. Christ transforms the useless into useful. What can He do in our lives?

Questions to ask yourself: Has Christ made a difference in my life? Have my old ways changed? Is there evidence of a transformed life? Am I looking to Christ to work powerfully in my life, or am I trying to change on my own power and strength? Do I see hope in others? Do I just look at them as who they used to be, or do I see who God can transform them to be? We must recognize that God is able to make a difference in our lives. We do not need to stay the same. God can clean us up and give us joy and purpose and direction. In Christ we are no longer useless because God's transforming power in our lives makes us useful.

3. Aristarchus—Willing to Do the Tough Stuff

When the going gets tough, what do you do? Do you step up to the plate, or do you run away? I wish I could say I've always been strong and courageous, but I haven't always persevered that well, at least not like Aristarchus. Now from this short mention of Aristarchus you don't see much about him, but let me give you a further introduction to this champion of courage and perseverance. Paul simply said, "My fellow prisoner Aristarchus sends you his greetings," but there is a myriad of stories packed into that one name.

First of all we see that Aristarchus is a fellow prisoner of Paul's, so he too is suffering for the sake of the gospel of Christ. We know from other scriptures that Aristarchus was with Paul on his third missionary journey, and he was seized with Paul by a rioting mob in Ephesus (Acts 19:29). He was with Paul and Tychicus in Greece (Acts 20:4) and also sailed with Paul to Rome (Acts 27:2), enduring both storm and shipwreck. We can say for certain that he did not live a dull life. Aristarchus didn't run from danger; he actually seems to have run to it! Where did his courage come from? Christ was his inspiration. He was sold out to his Savior.

Questions to ask yourself: How far am I willing to go for Christ? Will I take a stand for Him even when it is unpopular? Am I willing to suffer persecution or ridicule because I follow Christ? Will I stand by others who take a stand for Him? Where does my courage come from? God's words to Joshua also gave great strength as he was about to face the coming battles. "Do not let this Book of the Law depart from your mouth; meditate on it day and night, so that you may be careful to do everything written in it. Then you will be prosperous and successful. Have I not commanded you? Be strong and courageous. Do not be terrified; do not be discouraged, for the LORD your God will be with you wherever you go."[4] Remember, you are not alone. You have a great and mighty God who is with you and will strengthen you. Stand on the foundation of His Word as your guide.

4. Mark, the Cousin of Barnabas—Overcame Rejection and Learned from His Mistakes

We all mess up, we all make mistakes, we all make wrong choices. The question is, Where will we go from there? Will we beat ourselves up in our minds and tell ourselves what failures we are? Or will we learn from our wrong turns, strengthen ourselves, and move forward? There is always hope. No mistake is too great that God can't redeem and bring something good through the trial. I'm sure Mark felt like a failure when

Paul rejected him. The whole story is not told here in Colossians, but we can easily put together the pieces. Here's all Paul wrote in the salutation concerning Mark in Colossians,

> *My fellow prisoner Aristarchus sends you his greetings, as does Mark,*
> *the cousin of Barnabas. (You have received instructions about him; if*
> *he comes to you, welcome him.)* [5]

Now for the rest of the story. Years earlier, Mark had started out along with Barnabas on Paul's first missionary journey, but he disappointed Paul by leaving in the middle of the journey. We don't know why he left. Later, when Barnabas wanted to bring Mark along on another of Paul's missionary journeys, Paul flatly refused to have Mark join them. He felt so strongly about it that Barnabas (the encourager) went one direction with Mark, while Paul went another direction without them. Now that's one big-time rejection! But Mark did not give up. He continued to work with Barnabas and later with Peter (Acts 12:12-13; 1 Peter 5:13). Eventually Mark and Paul reconciled, and he became one of Paul's fellow workers (Philemon 24). Paul encourages the Colossians to welcome Mark, and later in his second letter to Timothy he warmly writes, "Get Mark and bring him with you, because he is helpful to me in my ministry."

Mark went from rejection to affection in Paul's eyes. The key is that he did not give up. He learned and grew from his mistakes of the past and proved and established his loyalty. Just as Paul forgave Mark, it looks like Mark also forgave Paul. If you had been publicly rejected by Paul, how would you handle it? There would be a tendency to become bitter and angry and say, "Well, if that's the way you feel about me, I'm done with you." But Mark must have had a teachable spirit with his eyes on Christ, not on Paul. Paul wasn't his focus, Christ was. When we are rejected, we must face our disappointments by turning our eyes back on Christ and His plan for us and getting our eyes off the rejection. By the way, this very same Mark is the one who wrote the Gospel of Mark. He was certainly an overcomer!

Questions to ask yourself: How do I handle rejection? Do I idolize acceptance and approval? Am I willing to turn to Christ and trust His plan for my life? Do I learn from my mistakes or only grow discouraged and bitter through them? We can choose how we handle the rejections of life. Remember God's sovereignty. Your rejection may be a surprise to you, but it is not to God. He has a plan—it may be just a little different than what you thought it would be. Trust Him, and ask Him to lead you and help you learn from each mistake. Grow through the disappointments and don't quit.

5. Jesus Justus—A Comforting Friend

The name *Jesus* was a common name in Paul's day. Paul identified Jesus Justus in the salutation here, but we do not see his name mentioned anywhere else in Scripture. Paul wrote,

> *Jesus, who is called Justus, also sends greetings. These are the only Jews among my fellow workers for the kingdom of God, and they have proved a comfort to me.*[6]

The name *Justus* was Roman and was a common name or surname denoting obedience and devotion to the law. Paul had suffered a great deal from the persecution of the legalistic Jews. They campaigned against him everywhere, but here was one who had chosen to follow Christ and was now a faithful friend.

A faithful friend formerly from the enemy camp, Justus was a comfort to Paul as well as a fellow worker. Strong, confident, forceful Paul needed the comfort of friends. It is interesting to note that this Greek word for *comfort* is not used anywhere else in the New Testament. It was a common medical term, from which our English word *paregoric* is derived, meaning a soothing drug. Justus was a friend who soothed Paul's soul and gave him emotional support and strength. God did not make us to be islands. We need connection. God provided a dear friend to be a refreshment to Paul in challenging times.

Questions to ask yourself: What kind of friend am I? Do I bring healing and comfort through my words and actions? Or am I a constant drain on others by my complaining and whining? Do I have friends who bring refreshment to my soul? Am I trying to live independently of others, or do I encourage connection and comfort through friendships? Look around you and consider the people God has placed in your life. Look for ways you can be a soothing balm in their life. Open the doors of your heart to let refreshing friends minister to you as well. And never underestimate the power of God to transform a former enemy into a heartfelt friend.

6. Epaphras—A Faithful and Devout Prayer Warrior

Who could you call or e-mail right now with a prayer request and know they would actually pray for you? It is wonderful to have a devout friend who is a woman of God and a woman of prayer. They not only inspire us, but they are a blessing to us. Epaphras was that sort of person. He was a leader in the church at Colossae and most likely in the one at Laodicea too, and he apparently traveled all the way to Rome to seek out Paul and talk with him about the challenges he was facing with the Gnostic influences. Paul was impressed not only by Epaphras' passion for God's Word, but also by his prayerful concern for his fellow Colossians. Here's what Paul wrote about him,

> Epaphras, who is one of you and a servant of Christ Jesus, sends greetings. He is always wrestling in prayer for you, that you may stand firm in all the will of God, mature and fully assured. I vouch for him that he is working hard for you and for those at Laodicea and Hierapolis.[7]

What an honorable mention here. Paul pats Epaphras on the back as "a servant of Christ Jesus." Epaphras was devoted to the cause of Christ to the point that he ended up in prison with Paul. Yes, we see in Paul's letter to Philemon that he calls Epaphras his "fellow prisoner." We don't know the whole story, but we do know of his commitment to preach and teach the gospel, which probably made the Jews his enemies, just like Paul. I think it is impressive that he is known for the way he struggled in prayer for the Colossians. Have you ever struggled in prayer for a person to come to know Christ or grow deeper in their faith? At times, God has put certain people on my heart for whom I fervently pray. It is a joy to go to the Father on someone else's behalf, and it is an increased joy when you see God work in their lives. Epaphras served faithfully as a pastor and a prayer warrior, and he sincerely cared about the spiritual condition of his fellow believers.

Questions to ask yourself: How devoted am I to the message of the gospel and to sharing it with others? How often do I struggle in prayer for another person? Do I have people in my life whom I consider devout and Christ-centered? Do I share my life and my prayer needs with them? Being a devoted Christian is not just for those who are in ministry. Each and every one of us can passionately pursue Christ by devoting time to prayer, studying His Word, and growing in fellowship with other people who are devoted to Him. Let us care enough for others to struggle for them in prayer.

7. Luke—Multitalented Man of God

People like Benjamin Franklin and Leonardo da Vinci have always fascinated me because they were gifted in a variety of different areas, and they used their many gifts for the betterment of mankind. Luke was that type of person. He was gifted in numerous skills, and he used those gifts and talents for the advancement of the kingdom of God. He even was a risk-taker, joining Paul on the famous storm-and-shipwreck journey to Rome. Here in the book of Colossians he gets only a brief mention, but there is so much more to this man. Paul included him saying, "Our dear friend Luke, the doctor, and Demas send greetings."[8]

Luke was a doctor and an adventurer, joining Paul on his missionary journey as well as sitting with him while he was a prisoner in Rome. Not only was he smart, but he was compassionate. Don't you wish all doctors were like him! He was a hard worker and a good friend. Luke was a careful and skillful writer—he wrote the Gospel of Luke and the book of Acts. In his Gospel, he portrayed the compassionate side of Christ, relaying stories of Christ's power and how He treated people with care and affection. We can read a little more about Luke because he included himself in some of the portions of Acts (chapters 16–28).

Paul was grateful for Luke's companionship and help. We know from the book of Acts that Paul was often brutally beaten and cast into prison, and I'm sure Luke was nearby to care for his injuries. Paul also had a "thorn in the flesh." We do not know what that means, but it was most likely some sort of physical ailment, and Luke was probably very helpful in his care of that as well. He was gifted both as a doctor and a writer and was open to using those gifts however God directed. God, in His kindness, moved in this talented man's heart to devote himself to service so Paul could benefit from his help, and the gospel was furthered in the process.

Questions to ask yourself: What gifts and talents has God given me? Am I open to how God wants to use those gifts for His glory? Who has God placed in my life as a gift to minister to my needs? Have I welcomed them in to my life? Have I thanked them? Are there any talents God is leading me to pursue? Am I willing to work hard using those gifts and talents? God has given us each something we can do. It may seem insignificant in our eyes, but it can be a true blessing to another person. It may be baking bread or mending clothes or typing letters, but each of us have something to offer. Let us be diligent to develop our skills and then ask God to direct us and guides us in how He wants us to use them.

8. Demas—Sad Story

In most lineups there is typically someone who seems good at first, but then turns out to be not so good after all. It happens on football teams, executive boards, and cheerleading squads. It even happened with the Big Twelve, Jesus' disciples. Judas was not destined to stay in the Big Twelve lineup. God has His purposes even in the disappointing examples in life. Often God uses these people as warning to us to guard us from following their path. Each of us are examples—let's just make sure we are good ones. In our Parting Ten lineup Paul mentions a man named Demas: "Our dear friend Luke, the doctor, and Demas send greetings." Demas is another one of those brief mentions here. He is also mentioned in Philemon as a "fellow worker." But in one of Paul's letters to Timothy we learn more. He wrote to Timothy saying, "Do your best to come to me quickly, for Demas, because he loved this world, has deserted me and has gone to Thessalonica."[9]

Sadly, when Paul needed him most, Demas deserted him. Why? Because he loved this world. I'm reminded of a parable Jesus told that mentions this same kind of love of the world. Jesus compared a plant that grew among the thorns to those who hear God's Word, but "the worries of this life and deceitfulness of wealth choke it, making it unfruitful."[10] In this world there are many distractions and tempting lures enticing us to fall in love with them rather than with Jesus. Having nice things and wealth is not wrong, but when we love them more than God and idolize them we become unfruitful. Let us heed the warning we learn from Demas and be aware of those things that may be tugging at our hearts and minds and leading us away from following Christ and loving Him with our whole heart.

Questions to ask yourself: What things of the world distract me and tug at my heart? In what ways are they keeping me from pursuing Christ? Do I need to make any changes in my life? How can I make Christ the center of my life? Unlike Mark, it seems as though Demas didn't learn from his mistakes. We do not know what became of him, but we can use his example to help open our eyes to the distractions around us and guard against replacing our love for the Lord with love for this world and the temporary delights it has to offer.

9. Nympha—Hostess with the Mostest

When my house is filled with people, I am thrilled. I may not be the world's best cook or housekeeper or decorator, but I can open my door with a smile and offer people a place to gather. From wedding showers to birthday parties to Bible studies, my home is well used, and it brings me great joy in the process. Nympha apparently had an open-door policy as well. Here's what Paul wrote next:

> *Give my greetings to the brothers at Laodicea, and to Nympha and the church in her house. After this letter has been read to you, see that it is also read in the church of the Laodiceans and that you in turn read the letter from Laodicea.*[11]

Opening our arms to others and welcoming them in the Lord gives us an opportunity to share Christ's love. In Romans we are told to "practice hospitality." The writer of Hebrews goes so far as to say, "Do not forget to entertain strangers, for by so doing some people have entertained angels without knowing it."[12] As for Nympha, she offered what she could to the Lord's work, opening up her home as a meeting place for the church. Let us all learn from her example and have open hearts and open homes. Let us be like the little boy with the five loaves of bread and two fish—he gave what he had, and God blessed it and used it for His people. We must be careful not to have such a tight grip on our stuff that we are not willing to use it to help others.

Paul greeted both Nympha, who hosted the Laodicean church in her home, and the general group of Laodicean believers. They were to be recipients of the Colossian letter after it was read in Colossae. The city of Laodicea was located a few miles northwest of Colossae. It was wealthy because of trade and commerce. You may remember Laodicea as the location of one of the churches addressed by the Lord in the book of Revelation. He described them as neither cold nor hot, but rather lukewarm. Sounds like the love of the world distracted them as well. Have you ever taken a sip of lukewarm water when you were hoping for something refreshing and cold? Then you know you want to simply spit it out of your mouth. That's what Jesus told the Laodiceans, but then He gave them this charge: "Be earnest, and repent. Here I am! I stand at the door and knock. If anyone hears my voice and opens the door, I will come in and eat with him, and he with me."[13] How do we keep from being lukewarm? Open up the door of your heart and invite Jesus in to fellowship and be the center of your life.

Questions to ask yourself: Do I have an open-door attitude when it comes to my home and things? Have I become lukewarm and lost my interest in the Lord? Am I being useful in His hands with what I have in *my* hands? No matter how much or how little we have, we can still have an attitude of hospitality. Consider others' needs, and look for ways to shine Christ's love through the things He has given you. What may seem little to you can be used in great ways for His work. Open the door to your home, but more importantly, open the door to your heart, inviting Christ to dwell and abide with you continually. As we abide in Him and He in us, we are never lukewarm.

10. Archippus—Finish Strong

If you have ever watched a long-distance race you can see the weariness in the runners' faces as they near the last quarter. I remember watching my own daughter Grace as she ran cross-country. I would cheer her on at the starting line, but then I would run forward to cheer her on when she was about three-quarters through the race. I'd always yell the same thing: "Finish strong!" There are times when we all grow weary. Paul encouraged the Galatians, "Let us not become weary in doing good, for at the proper time we will reap a harvest if we do not give up."[14] It's tempting to throw in the towel when you don't see results or when you are just plain tired. We all need a word of encouragement.

Paul ends his salutations with this word: "Tell Archippus: 'See to it that you complete the work you have received in the Lord.'"[15] In other words, don't throw in the towel; finish what the Lord has given you to do. Endure. We can use this reminder in our work because our work isn't always going to be fun. There are some long stretches where we may feel like giving up. We need to be encouragers of one another to keep going, stick with it, to not grow weary in God's work. Warren Wiersbe notes that "ministry is not something we do for God; it is something God does in and through us."[16] God has a work for each of us to do in this world. It may not be an official "ministry," but it is a work He wants us to fulfill, a work He has created us for and purposed us for. Let us continue to find our strength in Him as we carry out our calling.

Questions to ask yourself: What has God called me to do? Have I grown weary of it? Do I need to heed Paul's advice to finish strong? How can I be a cheerleader for others who may have grown weary? My dear sister in Christ, recognize that God created you for a purpose. He will equip you for that purpose, so keep your eyes on Him, and when you grow weary listen to Paul's voice saying, "Finish strong!" Look for opportunities to share those words with others who have grown weary. Persevere through the tough times and follow God's direction. In Corinthians we read, "My dear brothers, stand firm. Let nothing move you. Always give yourselves fully to the work of the Lord, because you know that your labor in the Lord is not in vain."[17]

A Final Word

A great lineup, wouldn't you agree? I'm glad we didn't skip the credits. I learned a significant life principle from each of these stories, and I hope you did too. Paul finishes his book with one last charge: "I, Paul, write this greeting in my own hand. Remember my chains. Grace be with you." *Remember my chains*. As we are busy about our lives and daily routines, it is easy to forget those who serve in ministry and who are being persecuted for the cause of Christ. Persecution of believers is not something that happened only in biblical times, it is happening right now in various places in the world.

Please pray for those who are risking their lives every day for the sake of Christ. You may not know their names or their specific needs, but God does. Voice of the Martyrs aids Christians around the world who are being persecuted for their faith in Christ. (You can learn more about modern-day martyrs by going to www.persecution.com.) Also, I encourage you to help missionaries both locally and abroad with your prayers and financial support. There may be missionaries who are supported through your church, or you can connect with them through a number of different organizations, such as Campus Crusade, Wycliffe Bible Translators, or Youth With A Mission (YWAM).

Confident Steps

ADDITIONAL READING: 1 Corinthians 12—Using our gifts to build the body of Christ

BATTLE FOR THE TRUTH:

Confidence Defeater—*I don't have anything to offer this world.*

Confidence Builder—God has equipped each and every one of us with gifts and talents, and our confidence soars as we use them to lift up others.

CHOICES:

- Be a loyal and faithful person.

- Allow God to transform you into a useful person for God's kingdom.
- Be strong and courageous. Don't run from the tough stuff.
- Learn from your mistakes and rejections. Trust God's plan and keep growing and going.
- Be a "soul refreshment" to your friends.
- Devote yourself to spending more time in prayer and to God's Word.
- Develop your gifts and talents and use them for kingdom purposes.
- Don't get distracted by the world.
- Open the doors of your heart and your home.

DELIBERATE PLAN: Can you relate?

Look back over the Parting Ten and think about which person impressed you the most. In other words, who was your hero in the lineup of the Parting Ten (well, actually Parting Nine, because Demas is not really a hero figure)? Circle the story in your book and examine the "questions to ask yourself" paragraph at the end of their story. Write down the answers to the questions in the spaces below as a form of journaling. Be open and honest with yourself. Write down one positive step you will take as a result of this self-evaluation.

_____

_____

_____

_____

Positive step forward: _____

_____

$\mathcal{S}$tepping Out in Confidence!

*"The LORD will be your confidence
and will keep your foot from being snared."*

Proverbs 3:26

*"Walk boldly and wisely...
There is a hand above that will help you on."*

Philip James Bailey

At the age of 17 Kristen Anderson felt as though she could no longer face the emotional pain she was dealing with inside, so in a moment of desperation she lay down on the railroad tracks in front of an approaching train, trying to end her life. Her legs were severed, and she lost eight pints of blood (people are supposed to die after they lose five pints). Yet miraculously she lived. Everyone kept telling her that God must have saved her for a reason, but she couldn't begin to understand why God would have saved her. At least not until she came to know Christ in a very real and personal way. Kristen had always known about God and even went to church, but she never knew she could have a personal and meaningful relationship with Him. As she grew to know Him, love Him, and follow Him, Christ began to change this despairing teen into a confident and joyful young lady.

In her book, *Life, In Spite of Me,* Kristen shares her powerful story of finding extraordinary hope as she worked through the emotional pain in her life as well as the physical challenges of losing her legs. She now shares the message of God's love, hope, and strength through her ministry called Reaching You (www.reachingyou.org), which reaches out to those who are dealing with emotional pain. Kristen even had the privilege of sharing her story on *The Oprah Winfrey Show* and was able to talk about her hope in Christ and the difference a relationship with Him makes. Kristen is a radiant woman who confidently reflects the love of Christ. Here's what she wrote in her book about a time after she accepted Christ and began to grow in her relationship with Him:

> As I prayed, I felt that I needed to let God be my best friend, I needed to talk to him about everything, and I needed to listen to him and make him a priority. Over the next few weeks, I started practicing that. When problems came up, I talked to God about them. And the more I did, the more I felt him with me...When I was worried, I'd pray and I'd feel more peace. The changes weren't big on the outside, but I could feel them on the inside. And I felt God, too. The more I focused on him, the more I realized that having a better relationship with him was what I had always needed, longed for. Seeing how this one thing helped me made me want to change more.[1]

Kristen learned the secret to confident living. It wasn't in having the perfect body or in having the perfect circumstances or the perfect people surrounding her, it came from having a vibrant relationship with the Perfect God who had created her. He is the secret. He is our confidence and our hope. He is able to transform our lives, just as He transformed Kristen's life. The apostle Peter wrote, "His divine power has given us everything we need for life and godliness through our knowledge of him who called us by his own glory and goodness. Through these he has given us his very great and precious promises, so that through them you may participate in the divine nature and escape the corruption in the world caused by evil desires."[2]

Yes, His divine power gives us everything we need for life and godliness through our knowledge of Him. It is my hope that as we have studied Colossians together you have come to know more about Christ and have gained an increased desire to know Him even more personally. The term Peter used for "knowledge" is actually *epignosis*, which denotes an intense investigation. It is not just knowing about Christ, but really knowing Him in a rich and meaningful way. As He enriches our lives we develop a God-confidence that focuses on Him and not on us.

Where's Your Confidence?

We must ask ourselves, "In whom do I place my confidence?" If my focus is on myself I can have the tendency to get down on myself. When our thoughts are on ourselves we tend to remember our mistakes, our hurts, our shortcomings. Our confidence sinks when we focus on our own foibles. The truth is, we all have made foolish decisions and bad choices. We have all screwed up a time or two, and that's why focusing on ourselves only brings us down. Trying to think positive thoughts about ourselves is only a temporary measure, and it still places our confidence on shaky ground. There are some women who struggle with pride, which is also a self-focused, short-lived dependence on self rather than on God.

True, unshakable confidence comes only from one source, the unshakable God who loves us. When we recognize that in Him we are forgiven and transformed, we are strengthened on the inside. As we look to Him for direction, we begin moving down new paths with confidence instead of indecision. And of course as we cast our cares, worries, and fears on the One who loves us, we walk with a peace that passes all understanding. When we fall in love with Him, we live in the confidence that we are never alone and that we are dearly loved.

You are hidden *in* Christ, not hidden *from* Him. He loves you and desires to be your strength. In the Old Testament, God spoke through the prophet Isaiah to remind His people of the love and strength He gives those who hope in the Lord.

"To whom will you compare me?
Or who is my equal?" says the Holy One.

Lift your eyes and look to the heavens:
Who created all these?
He who brings out the starry host one by one,
and calls them each by name.
Because of his great power and mighty strength,
not one of them is missing.

Why do you say, O Jacob,
and complain, O Israel,
"My way is hidden from the Lord;
my cause is disregarded by my God"?

Do you not know?
Have you not heard?
The Lord *is the everlasting God,*
the Creator of the ends of the earth.
He will not grow tired or weary,
and his understanding no one can fathom.

He gives strength to the weary
and increases the power of the weak.
Even youths grow tired and weary,
and young men stumble and fall;
but those who hope in the Lord
will renew their strength.
They will soar on wings like eagles;
they will run and not grow weary,
they will walk and not be faint. [3]

The woman who places her hope in the Lord will soar like an eagle. She will run and not grow weary; she will walk and not faint. It doesn't mean that life will go smoothly in every situation, and it doesn't mean we will get everything we want in life. It means that God will give us the strength and peace we need to live confidently in both the good times and the bad. We have no promise that life will be perfect, but we are promised that God will never leave us even through the storms in life. The secret to confident living is placing our hope in Him and not in ourselves. Let's take a brief look at several great men and women of faith in Scripture who found their hope in God. Listen to their hearts as they find their strength and help in the Lord.

Moses and Miriam wrote these words after God miraculously parted the Red Sea and the Israelites walked across on dry land: "The LORD is my strength and my song; he has become my salvation. He is my God, and I will praise him, my father's God, and I will exalt him. The LORD is a warrior; the LORD is his name."[4]

Deborah, a brave leader in Israel, found strength in God and not man to save the Israelites in battle. She wrote a song after the battle in which she declared, "May all who love you be like the sun when it rises in its strength."[5]

Ruth chose to place her dependence on the Lord and not in comfort of her homeland after her husband died. Although she was not an Israelite, she pledged to trust the Lord God and follow Him as her God. In a pronouncement of faith she said to her Israelite mother-in-law, "Your God will be my God."[6]

Hannah, childless and feeling worthless, knew it was the Lord who made her strong. She prayed to Him, and God heard her prayers.

> *My heart rejoices in the LORD!*
> *The LORD has made me strong.*
> *Now I have an answer for my enemies;*
> *I rejoice because you rescued me.*
> *No one is holy like the LORD!*
> *There is no one besides you;*
> *There is no Rock like our God.*[7]

Young David boldly fought against Goliath with only a sling shot and five stones. He placed his confidence in God even as a young boy while guarding sheep in the wilderness. David said, "You have been my hope, O Sovereign LORD, my confidence since my youth. From birth I have relied on you; you brought me forth from my mother's womb. I will ever praise you."[8]

David went on to lead Israel into many victorious battles as he depended on God for guidance and deliverance:

The LORD is my light and my salvation—
Whom shall I fear?
The LORD is the stronghold of my life—
Of whom shall I be afraid?
When evil men advance against me
To devour my flesh,
When my enemies and my foes attack me,
They will stumble and fall.
Though an army besiege me,
My heart will not fear,
Though war break out against me,
Even then will I be confident. [9]

David's psalms overflow with a message of strength in the Lord. Here's one of the many passages we can read about David's God-confidence:

Praise be to the LORD,
for he has heard my cry for mercy.
The LORD is my strength and my shield;
my heart trusts in him, and I am helped.
My heart leaps for joy
and I will give thanks to him in song. [10]

Before we move on to hear from David's son, I just want you to notice how this passage ends. Yes, giving thanks to God. Looks like God is trying to tell us something. This is a good reminder that a confident woman is not only one who wholeheartedly trusts in the Lord and experiences great joy, but she is also a woman who overflows with thanksgiving to Him.

Solomon, the wisest man who ever lived, would have been tempted to place his confidence in his own abilities, yet he recognized his confidence needed to be founded and grounded in the Lord. He said, "In the fear of the LORD one has strong confidence, and his children will have a refuge."[11] He also encouraged us to not be filled with worry and fears, but instead he told us, "Have no fear of sudden disaster or of the ruin that overtakes the wicked, for the LORD will be your confidence and will keep your foot from being snared."[12]

Jeremiah, who bravely served God through suffering, betrayal, and imprisonment, found his confidence in the Lord. He proclaimed, "Blessed are those who trust in the LORD and have made the LORD their hope and confidence."[13]

Mary, the mother of Jesus, humbly recognized all God had done in her life. Her song of praise and thanksgiving to Him certainly reflects the heart of a woman who has found her joy in Him.

> *My soul glorifies the Lord*
> *and my spirit rejoices in God my Savior,*
> *for he has been mindful*
> *of the humble state of his servant.*
> *From now on all generations will call me blessed,*
> *for the Mighty One has done great things for me—*
> *holy is his name.*
> *His mercy extends to those who fear him,*
> *from generation to generation.* [14]

Even the powerful apostle Paul found his confidence in Christ, not himself. As he talked about his own ministry he said, "Such confidence as this is ours through Christ before God. Not that we are competent in ourselves to claim anything for ourselves, but our competence comes from God."[15]

Are you catching the great truth that we have heard from each of these faith-filled men and women? Their eyes were on God as they depended on Him, not on themselves, in every area of life. Through their difficulties, disappointments, and joys, they found their hope in the Lord, looking to Him for their strength. Not one of them had a perfect life. It's easy to think we will have confidence...

...*if* I have the right job.

...*if* I get married.

...*if* I have a better body.

...*if* I further my education.

...*if* I could have a better wardrobe.

...*if* my kids were high-achievers.

...*if* I were good at something.

What is your big "if"? Where are you looking for your confidence? These things listed above may be well and good, and God may be leading you to pursue some of these goals. I'm not saying these pursuits are wrong—I am just saying that if you are finding your identity and hope in those things, then you are setting yourself up for disappointment. When you find your identity in Christ, you are building your life on a solid-rock foundation that is unshakable.

Who Are You?

In this book we have learned who Christ is, and we have also learned who you are as a follower of Him. Let's review what we know about Christ.

- He is the exact image of the Invisible God.
- He is above all creation.
- He created all things in heaven and on earth.
- All things are made by Him and for Him.
- He is before all things, He has always existed.
- By Him all things hold together.
- He is the head of the church.
- All the fullness of the deity dwells in Him.
- He reconciled us to God through His death on the cross.
- He rose from the dead (the firstborn from among the dead).
- He is the head over every power and authority.

Who are you? As a follower of Christ...

- You are created by Him, formed and fashioned by the One who has always existed.

- You are rescued from the dominion of darkness.
- You are a citizen of God's kingdom.
- You are redeemed (bought for a price through Christ's death).
- You are holy in His sight.
- You are without blemish.
- You are free from accusation.
- Christ dwells in you. He is your hope of glory.
- You are complete (satisfied, filled up) in Him.
- You are alive with Christ.
- You are hidden in Christ, secure in Him.
- You are a new creation in Christ; the old self is gone.
- You have received beautiful new clothes of righteousness to wear.
- You are being renewed in knowledge in the image of your Creator.
- You are one of God's chosen people.
- You are holy and dearly loved.

We know who we are because we know what Christ did. What a wonderful foundation on which to stand! We stand on Christ our solid rock. He did for us what we could not do for ourselves. The more we know Him and understand His sovereignty and power, love and kindness, mercy, and forgiveness, the greater our confidence grows in Him. Jeremiah encouraged the Israelites to be careful about boasting in their own accomplishments. Instead he said they ought to boast in the fact that they knew and understood God. Here's the message God gave him:

> This is what the Lord says: "Let not the wise man boast of his wisdom or the strong man boast of his strength or the rich man boast of his riches, but let him who boasts boast about this: that he understands

and knows me, that I am the LORD, *who exercises kindness, justice and righteousness on earth, for in these I delight," declares the* LORD.[16]

In your mind, what do you tend to boast about? Examine for a moment what kinds of things you feel give you your bragging rights. Where do you pat yourself on the back or tend to think you are better than others? Now think about it—can you boast that you know the Lord? This is the one area in life we ought to boast about! We should brag in this one area, that we understand and know the Lord who exercises kindness, justice, and righteousness. God delights in this kind of boasting.

What Has He Given You to Do?

When Rosie Lee Butler came to know Christ, her excitement was contagious. The truth about what Christ had done on the cross and the fact that she was redeemed in Him truly changed her life. She began asking the Lord how she could reach out and share her joy in Christ with the people in her neighborhood. God placed in her heart the desire to reach out to the children in the neighborhood to let them know that God loved them and had a plan for their lives. How do you get kids interested in coming to your house to learn about God's love and His Word? You cook for them!

Rosie Lee served everything from cookies to lemonade to hot dogs and chili. The kids came, and they stayed to hear the messages that Rosie Lee shared about Jesus Christ. Rosie Lee didn't go to seminary, and she was not a Bible scholar, but she knew God's love and knew how to share God's truth from the Bible. She faithfully taught, and the kids gladly came week after week. Many kids came to know Christ in a very real way through Rosie Lee's faithful Bible teaching. Even more beautiful is the fact that a number of those kids went on to become preachers and missionaries. God used Rosie Lee's enthusiasm and faithfulness in her own little home to affect hundreds, maybe thousands, around the globe.

Rosie Lee didn't focus on what she couldn't do, she focused on what she could do. She could cook, she could teach from the Bible, and she could invite people to her home. What can you do? What gifts has God given you? We are not all like Rosie Lee, but we all do have something God has given us. He has given us gifts we can use for something greater than ourselves; gifts to use for God's kingdom. Throughout Scripture we are encouraged to use our gifts to love and serve others. Perhaps you feel as though you do not have anything to give. You can begin by focusing on others' needs and sincerely loving them.

The apostle Peter reminded us of what we can do when he wrote,

> *Above all, love each other deeply, because love covers over a multitude of sins. Offer hospitality to one another without grumbling. Each one should use whatever gift he has received to serve others, faithfully administering God's grace in its various forms. If anyone speaks, he should do it as one speaking the very words of God. If anyone serves, he should do it with the strength God provides, so that in all things God may be praised through Jesus Christ. To him be the glory and the power forever and ever. Amen.* [17]

When we pour ourselves into loving God and loving others, we begin to blossom and grow as confident women. The cure to boredom and frustration with yourself is to get up and get out and do something for someone else. As a woman who stands firm because you know who you are in Christ, you can step out with confidence as you use your gifts for a greater purpose in this world. Jesus said, "Let your light shine before men, that they may see your good deeds and praise your Father in heaven."[18]

A Confident Perspective

The Valley of Vision is a collection of Puritan prayers and devotions from the early 1600s compiled by Arthur Bennett. In it you find deep, heartfelt, and honest prayers filled with love and conviction. One especially stands out to me as a fitting close to our study of Colossians and our journey to confidence. Read it slowly and thoughtfully and contemplate the words. I especially love it because it so eloquently speaks of the beauty of knowing Christ and what He means to us. It's called "The Life Look."

O God,
I bless thee for the happy moment
When I first saw thy law fulfilled in Christ,
Wrath appeased, death destroyed, sin forgiven,
    my soul saved.
Ever since, thou hast been faithful to me:
Daily have I proved the power of Jesus' blood,
Daily have I known the strength of the Spirit,
My teacher, director, sanctifier.
I want no other rock to build upon than that I have,
Desire no other hope than that of gospel truth,
Need no other look than that which gazes on the cross.
Forgive me if I have tried to add anything to the one
    foundation,
If I have unconsciously relied upon my knowledge,
Experience, deeds, and not seen them as filthy rags,
If I have attempted to complete what is perfect in Christ;
May my cry be always, Only Jesus! Only Jesus!
Fullness in his righteousness
Eternal vitality in his given life,
Indissoluble union in fellowship with him;
In him I have all that I can hold;
Enlarge me to take in more.
If I backslide,
Let me like Peter weep bitterly and return to him;
If I am tempted, and have no wit,
Give me strength enough to trust in him;
If I am weak,
May I faint upon his bosom of eternal love;
If in extremity,
Let me feel that he can deliver me;
If driven to the verge of hope and to the pit of despair,
grant me grace to fall into his arms.
O God, hear me, do for me more
Than I ask, think, or dream.[19]

May this prayer serve as an encouragement for your own heartfelt, personal prayers to the Almighty God who lavishes His love upon you. Let us look only to Jesus for our confidence and satisfaction. There is no surer foundation on which to build our lives. Our lives can be full and rich with meaning because He is at the center. Joy and peace are ours because He loves us and forgives us. Strength undergirds us in times of trouble, for He is our rock. We can cry in His arms, for He is our comfort, and we can smile at the future because He is our hope.

It is my hope that this book has strengthened you as a person as you have come to know the God who loves you in a deeper and richer way. I hope that as you have been strengthened with confidence on the inside, you will stand a little taller with confidence on the outside. He created you and formed you from your mother's womb. He makes no mistakes. You are dearly loved by Him, and through your faith in Christ you have been reconciled to Him, forgiven, made to be without blemish, no longer accused. He has transformed your old life into a new life. He has equipped you with gifts to bless this world, and He will give you the power, ability, and direction to use those gifts. Don't listen to the lies of the enemy that will drain your confidence—rather, grow deeper still in your relationship with the God who loves you. This book was the diving board, so to speak—now jump in with both feet and drench yourself in His unfailing love.

Confident Steps

ADDITIONAL READING: Psalm 34—Boast in the Lord

Confidence Defeater: *I am alone. My confidence comes from depending on my own abilities and circumstances.*

Confidence Builder: Unshakable confidence comes from placing our hope in the Lord, and not in ourselves or other people.

CHOICES:

- Put your hope and trust in the Lord.
- Allow joy and thankfulness to overflow from your confidence.
- Grow to know Christ in a deeper and more personal way.
- Do not fear the future; let the Lord be your confidence.
- Use the gifts God has given you to be a blessing to the people around you.
- Step out and shine His light.

DELIBERATE PLAN: Unshakable confidence.

Take some time for an honest evaluation of your confidence and consider what you currently are placing your hope in to help you feel good about yourself. Prayerfully ask the Lord to reveal any areas of false confidence that draw you away from true confidence in Christ and write them below. Typical areas in which we tend to put our confidence are...

- career, volunteer status, or hobbies
- husband or boyfriend
- children's accomplishments
- looking perfect (body and clothing)
- peaceful circumstances
- good health
- friends
- status
- money
- the things money can buy
- higher education
- personal achievements or abilities
-
-

•

•

•

Now I want to encourage you to lay that false sense of confidence at the Lord's feet. Recognize that these things or people cannot provide sure footing for your foundation of hope. Ask the Lord to help you place your hope in Him alone.

> *Father, You are my rock and my fortress. There is no surer foundation than You. Father, forgive me when I place my confidence in _____ and try to find my hope in it. Help me to recognize areas in my life that offer false hope. Help me to find my hope and confidence in Christ alone, for it is in Him that I live and move and have my being. Keep my eyes on You, O Lord. You are my eternal, unchangeable, immovable source of strength. In Jesus' name I pray, amen.*

$\mathscr{D}$iscussion Questions

If you are planning to use this book for a group study, you may find it helpful to use the following discussion questions. Keep in mind there is also a coordinating six-session video available in which I open up the lesson for you as I bring additional information and stories to your study. You can also go to my website for a free download of tips to help you lead a discussion group.

I'm thankful you have chosen to study this book. May God bless you on your journey to confident living.

Part One: Transform Your Thinking

Chapter One: Where in the World Is Truth?

1. Why is it important to know your own personal philosophy or worldview?

2. What does it mean to have a biblical worldview?

3. In what ways does it strengthen your confidence to establish your foundation on the Bible?

4. What philosophies that seem opposed to a biblical worldview are prevalent in our culture?

5. Share about a time in your life when a passage from the Bible gave you strength or direction for yourself.

Chapter Two: Powerful Prayers You'll Want to Pray (Colossians 1:1-14)

1. How does it improve a relationship with someone when you spend time thanking God for that person?

2. Do you have someone who is a prayer warrior in your life?

3. What does it mean to spiritually "bear much fruit" and "grow in the knowledge of Christ"?

4. Have you come to a place of trusting Christ as your Savior—as the One who redeemed you and forgave you?

5. How does it strengthen your confidence to know you are rescued from the dominion of darkness and have been brought into the kingdom of the Son whom God the Father loves?

Part Two: Grow in Christ

Chapter Three: The Joy of Knowing Him (Colossians 1:15-20)

1. What do you learn about God when you look at the life of Jesus, since Jesus is the exact image of God?

2. What difference does it make in your confidence level to know you are created by Christ and for Him?

3. Share about a time in your life when you recognized Christ was holding your life together.

4. Why is it important to know that all the fullness of God dwelt in Jesus?

5. How has your understanding of Christ increased as you read this chapter?

Chapter Four: Embracing the Lover of Your Soul (Colossians 1:21-23)

1. How would you describe yourself before you came to know Christ?

2. What accusations from the enemy do you sometimes listen to in your mind?

3. How does it help you to know that you are "holy in His sight"?

4. Why is it difficult to believe we are without blemish?

5. What does it mean to have a faith that is "established and firm" in Christ?

Part Three: Step Forward

Chapter Five: Hidden Treasures and Hope-Filled Dreams (Colossians 1:24–2:5)

1. How can a person rejoice even in the midst of difficulties?

2. What does the statement, "Christ in you, the hope of glory" mean to you personally?

3. Why is it tempting to believe some of the fake treasures (popular philosophies) in our culture today? Why are they so intriguing to people?

4. What are ways people try to discover secrets of wisdom and knowledge outside of Christ?

5. What treasures of wisdom and knowledge do you find in Christ? How does that strengthen your confidence?

Chapter Six: Confidently Walking with Christ (Colossians 2:6-23)

1. What does it mean to be rooted in Christ?

2. In what ways does your life reflect Christ? In other words, in what ways are you built up in Him?

3. Does your life overflow with thankfulness? What steps can you take to be a more thankful person?

4. How can you actively strengthen your faith in Him?

5. In our culture today, what religious "add-ons" do you see people using to make themselves appear more spiritual?

Part Four: Be Your Best

Chapter Seven: Glorious Makeover (Colossians 3:1-11)

1. How can you continue to set your focus on things above?

2. Name some of the things on this earth that can be a distraction to the things above.

3. When you think about the church as the "bride of Christ," how does that strengthen your confidence in understanding who you are?

4. As we live with a focus on that glorious day when we will see Jesus face-to-face, why is it important to get rid of certain old rags in our life?

5. How does it change you as a person to live for His kingdom?

Chapter Eight: You Look Divine! (Colossians 3:12-17)

1. When you think of a lovely person, what inner qualities come to mind?

2. Which qualities do you want to be more intentional about putting on after reading this chapter?

3. What are some practical ways to allow the peace of Christ to rule your heart?

4. How do you plan to grow richer in the knowledge of God's Word?

5. Are there any changes you want to make in your life as you think about doing everything in the name of the Lord Jesus?

Part Five: Strengthen Your Relationships

Chapter Nine: How to Live with Those Closest to You (Colossians 3:18–4:1)

1. Why do rules of order make sense in a business, a school, or a home?

2. In your opinion, what is it that bothers women most about the word *submit*?

3. Describe what you think it means to "work whole-heartedly for the Lord."

4. What challenged you most in this chapter?

5. In what ways does a gentle and quiet spirit display power and strength? How is Jesus a good example of this?

Chapter Ten: Mastering Meaningful Conversations with God and Man (Colossians 4:2-6)

1. How has this chapter encouraged you to develop or grow in your prayer life?

2. Share about a time when you experienced an answer to prayer.

3. Why is it important to thank God continually?

4. Why do you think so many outsiders are turned off by Christians in our culture today?

5. What are some ways you can make your conversation seasoned with salt when you talk with those who do not know Christ?

Part Six: Shine with Joy

Chapter Eleven: Recognize the Blessing You Bring to This World—(Colossians 4:7-18)

1. In Paul's Parting Ten, who can you most relate to in your life?

2. What are ways you are currently using your gifts and talents?

3. How have you been challenged by the "questions to ask yourself" in each section?

4. As you read these stories, what does it show you about the variety of God's creation?

5. In what ways can you encourage the gifts of the people around you?

Chapter Twelve: Stepping Out in Confidence!

1. What touched you most about Kristen's story?

2. When you read the words of the faithful men and women throughout Scripture, what did you notice about their dependence on God?

3. When you look at the list that identifies who you are in Christ, how does it build your confidence?

4. What do you tend to place your confidence in other than Christ?

5. How has this book helped you find your identity in Him?

$\mathscr{E}$ndnotes

Chapter 1—Where in the World Is Truth?

1. John Piper, *Spectacular Sins* (Wheaton, IL: Good News Publishers, 2008), 57.
2. www.churchleader.net/Transforming/WorldviewDevelopment/tabid/119/Default.aspx.
3. Isaiah 40:8.
4. Psalm 19:7-11.
5. 2 Timothy 3:16.
6. Immanuel Kant. *Critique of Pure Reason,* rev. ed. (Stillwell, KS: Digireads.com Publishing, 2005), 312.
7. Used by permission of Myrtle Grove Christian School, Wilmington, NC. The definition and description of the school's worldview is adapted from Christian Overman and Don Johnson, *Making the Connections* (Puyallup, WA: The Biblical Worldview Institute, 2003).

Chapter 2—Powerful Prayers You'll Want to Pray

1. Psalm 103:13.
2. http://debbietaylorwilliams.com.
3. John 15: 10-11.
4. John 15:1-5.
5. Galatians 5:22-23.
6. Romans 3:23.
7. Romans 6:23.
8. If you would like to know more about the inheritance we have in Christ, call 1-888-NeedHim to talk with someone in person.

Chapter 3—The Joy of Knowing Him

1. 1 Timothy 1:17.
2. John 4:24.
3. John 1:17-18 NLT.

4. Genesis 1:26.

5. Psalm 103:17,8-12.

6. A.W. Tozer, *The Knowledge of the Holy* (New York: Harper, 1961), 44.

7. Tozer, 47.

8. Hank Hanegraaff, *The Complete Bible Answer Book* (Nashville, TN: Thomas Nelson Publishers, 2008), 126.

9. Psalm 121.

10. Leslie O'Hare. Leslie is television host of *The Leslie O'Hare Show,* aired on KFWD in Dallas, Texas. Her national women's magazine—"*L*" *The Leslie Magazine*—was scheduled to launch November 2010. Leslie's website is www.leslieoharemedia.com.

11. Psalm 37:23-24 NLT.

12. Acts 4:12.

13. Romans 8:10-11.

14. *More Gathered Gold,* John Blanchard, ed. (Hertfordshire, England: Evangelical Press, 1986), 120.

15. John 14:9-10.

16. Colossians 2:10.

17. John 3:16-18.

18. Ephesians 2:8-9.

Chapter 4—Embracing the Lover of Your Soul

1. *Gleanings from Sacred Poets* (London, England: Gall & Inglis, nd), 121.

2. Story from the "Gospel Herald," *Knight's Master Book of 4000 Illustrations,* Walter B. Knight, ed. (Grand Rapids, MI: Eerdmans Publishing, 1956), 390.

3. Romans 8:7-8.

4. Romans 8:1.

5. Romans 5:8-10 NLT.

6. Ephesians 3:16-21.

7. Edward Mote, 1797–1874, hymn "The Solid Rock."

Chapter 5—Hidden Treasures and Hope-Filled Dreams

1. *Gleanings from Sacred Poets* (London, England: Gall & Inglis, nd), 121.

2. Henri J.M. Nouwen, *With Open Hands* (Notre Dame, IN: Maria Press, 1972), 43.

3. 2 Corinthians 1:5.

4. Romans 5:2-5.

5. Ephesians 1:11-14 MSG.

6. Romans 11:33-36.

Chapter 6—Confidently Walking with Christ

1. John 8:31-32.

2. John 15:5 NKJV.

3. Ron Rhodes, *5-Minute Apologetics for Today* (Eugene, OR: Harvest House Publishers, 2010), 7.

4. Rhodes, 7.

5. John 14:6.

6. Pascal, *Pensees* #425.

7. Psalm 23:1 NLT.

8. *More Gathered Gold,* John Blanchard, ed. (Hertfordshire, England: Evangelical Press, 1986), 186.

Chapter 7—Glorious Makeover

1. Matthew 6:25-33 NLT.

2. J. Wilbur Chapman, first published 1911; music by Charles H. Marsh.

3. Ephesians 5:31-32.

4. 1 Corinthians 6:18-20.

5. James 1:14-15.

6. Timothy Keller, *Counterfeit Gods* (New York: Dutton, 2009), xiv.

7. Ephesians 4:26-32.

8. Romans 12:9-10,17-21.

9. Matthew 12:34-35.

10. See www.HopeHelpHeal.org.

Chapter 8—You Look Divine!

1. 1 Peter 5:6-7 NET.

2. Psalm 103:8.

3. Galatians 5:22-23.

4. 1 Corinthians 13:4-8.

Chapter 9—How to Live with Those Closest to You

1. Galatians 3:28.

2. N.T. Wright, *Paul for Everyone: The Prison Letters* (Louisville, KY: Westminster John Knox Press, 2004), 186.

3. John Phillips, *Exploring Colossians & Philemon* (Grand Rapids, MI: Kregel, Inc., 2002), 191.

4. We must also be careful not to overlabel emotional abuse. It is wise to seek biblical counselors if you feel you are in an emotionally abusive situation.

5. Henry Cloud and John Townsend, *It's Not My Fault* (Nashville, TN: Integrity Publishers, 2007).

6. Luke 2:49-52.

7. Tim Kimmel, *Grace-Based Parenting* (Nashville, TN: Thomas Nelson, 2005).

8. Proverbs 22:6.

9. *Speaker's Source Book II*, Glen Van Ekeren, ed. (Englewood Cliffs, NJ: Prentice Hall, Inc., 1994), 46.

10. *Speaker's Source Book*, 392.

11. *Speaker's Source Book*, 393.

12. *Knight's Master Book of New Illustrations,* Walter B. Knight, ed. (Grand Rapids, MI: Eerdmans Publishing, 1956), 746.

Chapter 10—Mastering Meaningful Conversations with God and Man

1. James 3:3-8.

2. www.gallup.com/poll/127721/few-americans-oppose-national-day-prayer.aspx.

3. *More Gathered Gold,* John Blanchard, ed. (Hertfordshire, England: Evangelical Press, 1986), 233.

4. Matthew 7:7-11 NLT.

5. Psalm 36:7-9.

6. Mark 14:34,37-38.

7. Psalm 50:14-15,23 NLT.

8. Luke 6:35.

9. Luke 17:17-19.

10. To learn more about Sharon Hill's ministry go to www.oncallprayer.org.

11. National Marriage Project at the University of Virginia, www.virginia.edu/marriageproject/.

Chapter 11—Recognize the Blessing You Bring to This World

1. Colossians 4:7-8.

2. Colossians 4:9.

3. Philemon 10-12.

4. Joshua 1:8-9.

5. Colossians 4:10.

6. Colossians 4:11.

7. Colossians 4:12-13.

8. Colossians 4:14.

9. 2 Timothy 4:9-10.

10. Matthew 13:22.

11. Colossians 4:15-16.

12. Hebrews 13:2.

13. Revelation 3:20-21.

14. Galatians 6:9.

15. Colossians 4:17.

16. Warren Wiersbe, *Be Complete* (Chicago: David C. Cook, 2008), 172.

17. 1 Corinthians 15:58.

Chapter 12—Stepping Out in Confidence!

1. Kristen Jane Anderson, *Life, In Spite of Me* (Colorado Springs, CO: Multnomah Books, 2010), 145.

2. 2 Peter 1:3-4.

3. Isaiah 40:25-31.

4. Exodus 15:2-3.

5. Judges 5:31.

6. Ruth 1:16 NLT.

7. 1 Samuel 2:1-2 NLT.

8. Psalm 71:5-6.

9. Psalm 27:1-3.

10. Psalm 28:6-7.

11. Proverbs 14:26 ESV.

12. Proverbs 3:25-26.

13. Jeremiah 17:7 NLT.

14. Luke 1:46-50.

15. 2 Corinthians 3:4-5.

16. Jeremiah 9:23-24.

17. 1 Peter 4:8-11.

18. Matthew 5:16.

19. *The Valley of Vision*, Arthur Bennett, ed. (Carlisle, PA: The Banner of Truth Trust, 1975), 96-97.

Notes

Notes

Notes

Notes

_____

_____

_____

_____

_____

_____

_____

_____

_____

_____

_____

_____

_____

_____

_____

_____

_____

_____

Notes

Notes

Notes

Notes

Notes

Notes

Notes

Notes

Karol Ladd is known as "the Positive Lady." Her heart's desire is to inspire and encourage women with a message of lasting hope and biblical truth. She is open, honest, and real in both her speaking and her writing. Formerly a teacher, Karol is the bestselling author of more than 25 books, including *A Woman's Passionate Pursuit of God, The Power of a Positive Mom,* and *The Power of a Positive Woman.* As a gifted communicator and dynamic leader, Karol is a popular speaker at women's organizations, church groups, and corporate events across the nation. She is a frequent guest on radio and television programs. Her most valued role is that of wife to Curt and mother to daughters Grace and Joy.

Find more information about Karol at:

Website: www.KarolLadd.com
Blog: www.ThriveDontSimplySurvive.wordpress.com
Twitter: karolladd
Facebook: Karol Ladd

A Woman's Passionate Pursuit of God
Creating a Positive and Purposeful Life

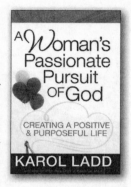

Resilient joy, consistent contentment, indescribable peace...you'll find all these in Paul's intriguing letter to the Philippians. As you explore it with popular author and speaker Karol Ladd, you'll catch her passion and infectious enthusiasm. You'll learn to live intentionally as you face life's daily challenges. Most important, you'll be helped to fall deeply in love with Jesus Christ, understand God's Word and His plans for your life, and say more and more, "Father, I want what You want."

Filled with inspiring true-life stories, practical steps, and study questions, this book is perfect for personal quiet times, as a book club pick, or for a group Bible study.

The DVD version of *A Woman's Passionate Pursuit of God* complements the book with six dynamic 30-minute sessions from Karol. A helpful leader's guide is included, and discussion questions are available through Karol's website—all of which makes this DVD excellent for small-group or church class study, as well as personal use.